THE SPIRITUAL COMBAT

LORENZO SCUPOLI

LORENZO Scupoli (c.1530-1610), was born in Otranto, Italy. He was admitted to the religious order of the Theatine Regular Clerks of St. Cajetan, in 1571, and by his desire, was called Lorenzo of Otranto. He later went to Milan, under the provost St. Andrew Avellino. After many years of active duties, he retired into strict seclusion and wrote *The Spiritual Combat.*

In 1589, the first edition of *Il combattimento spirituale* (The Spiritual Combat) appeared. The first edition contained thirty-three chapters, but Scupoli continued to add to the text, and it gradually grew into the current version containing sixty-six chapters. A separate book, *Aggiunta al combattimento spirituale* (Addition to the Spiritual Combat), along with *Modo di recitare la Corona della Madonna* (How to recite the rosary), are considered to be the last of his writings. Since its introduction, four centuries ago, approximately six hundred editions of *The Spiritual Combat* have been published globally.

SCRIPTORIA BOOKS

THE word "scriptoria" literally means "places for writing." Historically, scriptoria were writing rooms, areas set apart in some monasteries for the use of scribes, or copyists of the community, to faithfully create or reproduce books by hand. Their work was exacting, and great care was taken to ensure a high degree of copy fidelity.

Scriptoria Books continues in the traditions set forth in these communities long ago. Each new Scriptoria publication has been transcribed word for word from an original text, then edited, formatted, typeset, and proofread through each revision. Our procedures are not automated. Our editions are not facsimiles and do not contain OCR interpreted text. Our books are carefully created new editions of classic works.

Refracted through the mist of years,
How red my setting sun appears,
    How lurid looks this soul of mine!

Henry Wadsworth Longfellow, *Weariness*

Cover Art: *Winter Landscape* by Julius Klever (1850-1924)

THE SPIRITUAL COMBAT

CLASSIC EDITION

LORENZO SCUPOLI

Scriptoria Books

The Spiritual Combat: Classic Edition
Lorenzo Scupoli

Copyright © 2014

Every effort has been made to preserve the text and language (English – UK) of the original publication. Minor corrections to spelling, capitalization, and punctuation were based on the period in which the work was written. Adornments found in the original edition have been omitted.

The original short work of *The Spiritual Combat* was first published in Italy, 1589, and reached its present length of sixty-six chapters soon after Scupoli's death in 1610. Between 1589 and 1750, more than 250 editions of *The Spiritual Combat* existed in Europe alone. Approximately 600 editions have been published globally since 1589. This English edition was transcribed from the Rivingtons, London, publication.

The Spiritual Combat / by Lorenzo Scupoli. --Classic edition.
p. cm.
ISBN 9780615913476 (pbk)
1. Religion --Christian Life --Spiritual Warfare 2. Spiritual Life --Catholic Church.
I. Scupoli, Lorenzo (1530-1610).

Scriptoria Books
Mesa, Arizona USA

www.scriptoriabooks.com

CONTENTS

THE SPIRITUAL COMBAT

CHAPTER 1

In what Christian Perfection consists; and that the attainment of it involves a struggle, and of four things necessary for this conflict.

IF you wish, beloved in Christ, to reach the height of perfection, and by drawing near to your God to become one spirit with Him (and no aim can be imagined or expressed which is greater, or nobler than this), you must before all else gain a true idea of what constitutes genuine spiritual perfection.

There are many who have believed it to consist exclusively in outward mortification, in hair-shirts and disciplines, in long watchings and fastings, and in other bodily sufferings and chastisements.

Others again, and especially women, think that they have reached the climax of perfection, when they say many prayers, attend many services and offices, and are regularly at Church and at Communion.

Some indeed (and amongst this class not a few Religious persons who have withdrawn themselves from the world), persuade themselves that perfection entirely depends on the regular attendance at the Hours of prayer, on silence, solitude, and exact observance of Rule.

And thus, some in these, and others in those external actions suppose perfection to consist. But they are all deceived. For although these practices are sometimes means of gaining the spirit of perfection, and sometimes are its fruits, yet in no sense can it ever be said that true spiritual perfection consists in these.

Unquestionably they are means most efficacious for obtaining spirituality, when they are properly and discreetly employed; for by them we gain strength against our own sinfulness and frailty, we are fortified against the assaults and snares of our common enemies, and, in short, are provided with those spiritual helps, which are necessary to all the servants of God, and especially to those who have but lately entered His service.

They are also fruits of the Spirit in truly spiritual persons, who "keep under" the body because it has offended its Maker, and in order to keep it low and submissive to His commands; in those who live in solitude and silence in order to avoid even the least occasions of sin, and to have their conversation in Heaven, and who give themselves entirely to the Service of God and to works of mercy; who pray, and meditate upon the Life and Passion of Jesus Christ, not for the sake of curiosity and devotional feeling, but that they may gain deeper knowledge of their own corruptness and of God's Mercy and Goodness, and that they may be more and more inflamed with the love of God, and the hatred of themselves—following the Son of God by self-denial, and by taking the Cross upon their shoulders; who frequent the Holy Sacraments with the view of glorifying the Divine

Majesty, that they may be more closely united with God, and gain fresh strength against their enemies.

To others, however, who found perfection entirely on external practices, such works may bring greater ruin than open sins; not that these works are bad in themselves, for in themselves they are very good, but in consequence of the mistaken use which is made of them they have this sad result; because those who practice them are so wrapped up in what they do, that they leave their hearts a prey to their own evil inclinations and to the devices of Satan. He sees them wandering from the right path, and not only does he leave them to the enjoyment of these exercises, but lets them vainly fancy that they are roaming amidst the delights of Paradise, and persuade themselves that they are borne upwards even to the angelic choirs, and that they feel the Presence of God within them. Such persons sometimes are so absorbed in curious, deep, delightful thoughts, that they become as it were oblivious of the world and of all creatures, and appear to themselves rapt even to the third heaven.

But in how great an error these persons have entangled themselves, and how far they are distant from that true perfection which we seek, may easily be gathered from their lives and conversation. For in everything, whether it be great or small, they seek their own advantage, and like to be preferred before others; they are self-willed and opinionated, blind to their own faults, sharp-sighted for the faults of others, and severely condemn the sayings and doings of other men.

But if you touch only with your finger a certain vain reputation in which they hold themselves, and are pleased to be held by others; if you bid them discontinue any of their regular and formal devotions, they are at once angry and exceedingly disturbed.

And if God Himself visits them with trials and infirmities (which never come without His appointment or permission, and which are the tests of His servants' faithfulness), or if He permits them to be sorely persecuted in order that they may gain a true knowledge of themselves, and be brought back to the way of true perfection, immediately the false foundation is discovered, and the miserable condition of the proud heart is seen. For in all events, whether adverse or prosperous, they are unwilling to be resigned and to humble themselves under the mighty hand of God, acquiescing in His just though hidden judgments; neither will they, in imitation of the most lowly and patient Son of God, abase themselves below all creatures, and love the persecutors and enemies as dear friends, because they are the instruments of Divine Goodness, and work together for their mortification, perfection and salvation.

It is therefore quite evident, that all such persons are in great danger. For since the inward eye is darkened, by which they see themselves and their outward actions which are good, they attribute to themselves a high decree of perfection, and so, becoming more and more puffed up, they readily pass judgment upon others; yet they themselves need a special miracle of grace to convert them, for nothing short of that would have effect. It is more easy to convert and bring back an open sinner to the path of truth, than the man whose sin is hidden and mantled with the semblance of virtue.

You clearly and distinctly see, then, from what I have said, that the essence of the spiritual life does not lie in any of those things to which I have alluded. It consists in nothing else but the knowledge of the Divine Goodness and Greatness, of our own nothingness, and proneness to all evil; in the love of God and the hatred of self; in entire subjection not only to God Himself, but for the love of Him, to all creatures; in giving up our own will, and in completely resigning ourselves to the Divine Pleasure; moreover, in willing and doing all this with no other wish or aim than the glory and honor of God, the fulfillment of His Will because it is His Will, and because He deserves to be served and loved.

This is the law of love engraved on the hearts of His faithful servants by the hand of the Lord Himself.

This is the self-denial which is required of us.

This is His sweet yoke and light burden.

This is that obedience to which our Redeemer and Master calls us, both by word and example.

But if you aspire to such a pitch of perfection, you must daily do violence to yourself, by courageously attacking and destroying all your evil desires and affections. In great matters as well as in small, it is necessary, then, that you prepare yourself and hold yourself in readiness for this conflict, for he only will be crowned who was brave in the battle.

Doubtless this is the hardest of all struggles, because by fighting against ourselves, we are, at the same time, attacked by ourselves, and on that account the victory obtained in such a conflict will be of all others the most glorious and most dear to God.

Therefore, if you used every endeavor to mortify yourself, and to tread down your inordinate affections, inclinations, and rebellious passions, even in the smallest matters, you would be rendering to God a far greater and more acceptable service, than if whilst permitting some of your inclinations to remain unmortified, you scourged yourself until you bled, fasted more rigorously, and practiced an austerity greater than that of the hermits and saints of the desert, or converted souls by thousands.

For, although in itself the conversion of souls is dearer to God than the mortification of an irregular desire, yet it is not your duty to will and perform that which is in itself more excellent, but that which God before all else strictly desires and requires of you. For He doubtless seeks and desires of you self-conquest, and the thorough mortification of your passions, rather than that you, willfully leaving one of them alive in you, should perform in some other direction some greater and more notable service for His sake.

Now you see wherein the real perfection of a Christian lies, and that to obtain it you must enter upon a constant and sharp warfare against self; you must provide yourself with four very safe and highly necessary weapons, that you may win the palm, and be finally a conqueror in this spiritual conflict—these are:

Distrust of Self . . . . . I.
Trust in God . . . . . . II.
Spiritual Exercises . . . III.
Prayer . . . . IV.

Concerning all these, with God's help, we intend plainly and briefly to treat.

CHAPTER 2

Of Distrust of Ourselves.

DISTRUST of yourself is so necessary in the spiritual combat, that without it you may be assured that you will neither gain the desired victory, nor be able to overcome even the weakest of your passions. You must be firmly convinced in your mind that this is the case, for we are too prone through our natural corruption to make a false estimate of ourselves; so that, though we are absolutely nothing, we persuade ourselves that we are something, and presume without the slightest foundation on our own strength.

This fault is one which it is not easy to discover, yet it is very offensive in the sight of God. For He desires and loves to see in us a loyal acknowledgment of this most certain truth, that He Alone is the Source of all good, and that all virtue and grace descend from Him to us, and that from ourselves nothing can come, not even a good thought, which would be worthy of His approval.

Yet, although this most necessary self-distrust is itself the work of the Divine Hand, and is wont to be bestowed by God upon His friends, sometimes by means of holy inspirations, sometimes by sharp chastisements, sometimes by violent and almost insurmountable temptations, at other times by ways not understood by us, nevertheless it is His will that we also, as far as we can, should do our part; I will therefore propose to you four means, by which, relying chiefly on God's assistance, you may be able to acquire self-distrust.

The first is, to meditate upon and to recognize your own vileness and nothingness, and the fact that of yourself you can do no good thing, whereby to deserve an entrance into the Heavenly Kingdom.

The second is, to seek from the Lord with fervent and humble prayers this self-distrust; seeing it is His gift. In order to obtain it, you must not only acknowledge that you are destitute of it, but also that you are wholly unable of yourself to gain it.

In this way, present yourself again and again before the Divine Majesty, with the assurance that of His goodness He will grant your request; endure the delay, however long, which His providence may appoint, and persevere; and without doubt you shall obtain it.

The third is, to live in continual fear of yourself, of your own judgment, of your great proneness to sin; and of the countless enemies, against whom you are of yourself utterly powerless, of their great experience in this warfare, their wiles, their capability of transforming themselves into angels of light, their innumerable snares and traps which they secretly spread in the very way itself of holiness.

The fourth is, that as soon as you have had any fall, you should enter at once more deeply and more consciously into the consideration of your own feebleness. It was for this purpose God permitted you to fall, that, being warned inwardly by inspiration, by a clearer light than before, you might, knowing yourself well, learn to despise yourself, and to regard yourself as something vile and of no account, and to be willing that others should view you in the same light. Otherwise you will never attain to a virtuous self-distrust, which is based on genuine humility and experimental self-knowledge, such as that we have spoken of.

This self-knowledge is clearly necessary for any one who seeks to have union with the supreme Light and uncreated Truth, and this the Divine Mercy teaches to the proud and to the presumptuous commonly through their falls; suffering them to fall into some sin, which they thought there was no chance of their doing, so that, gaining in this experimental way self-knowledge, they may learn to distrust themselves in every respect.

But the Lord has not recourse to so miserable a remedy as this, until milder means have been tried, and have failed to work all the good the Divine goodness had in view.

He permits a man to fall more or less in proportion to his pride and self-esteem; so that if there were no presumption (as in the case of the Blessed Virgin Mary), there would be no fall.

Therefore, when you happen to have a fall, betake yourself at once to the humble consideration of what you are, and earnestly seek from the Lord the true Light whereby you may know yourself, and entirely distrust yourself, if you do not want to fall again, and perhaps the next time into deeper sin.

CHAPTER 3

Of Trust in God.

ALTHOUGH, as we have said, self-distrust is essential for this spiritual combat, nevertheless it alone would not be enough, for then we should fly from our enemies or be overcome by them. There is need to add to it perfect trust in God, in the hope and expectation that He Alone will vouchsafe to us every good thing we need—His help, and the victory.

From ourselves indeed, who are nothing, we can expect nothing but falls, for which cause we ought entirely to distrust ourselves; but, with the help of our Lord, we may be assured of success at all times; provided that to obtain His aid, we arm our hearts with a lively confidence in Him. Four means will help us to gain this.

First, by beseeching God to grant it to us.

Secondly, by keeping the eye of faith fixed on the immense Power and infinite Wisdom of God, with Whom nothing is either impossible or difficult; by considering that His Goodness is unbounded, and that His willingness and desire to give, each hour and moment, whatever may be needful for the spiritual life and for the entire mastery over self, is unbounded, if we with trustfulness fly for refuge to His arms.

For if our Divine Shepherd for thirty-three years followed after His lost sheep, with cries so piercing that His voice grew hoarse, through a road so rough and thorny that He shed all His blood upon it, and laid down His life, will He not now—when the poor sheep follows Him by obeying His commands, or at least with the desire of doing so (though sometimes feeble), when it calls upon Him and entreats Him, will He not now cast upon it the life-giving glance of His Countenance, hear its cry, lay it upon His Divine Shoulders, rejoicing with all His neighbors and with the Angels of Heaven?

For if our Lord in His love spared no pains in order to find the blind and dumb sinner, the lost coin of the Gospel, is it possible that He would turn away from one who, like a lost sheep, calls and cries piteously after the shepherd?

And can it be imagined, that God, Who knocks continually at the door of man's heart, that He might enter in and sup there, and communicate His gifts, would, when invited by man to enter into that heart, turn a deaf ear, and refuse to come in?

The third way of gaining this holy confidence in God, is to recall the truths of Holy Scripture where it will be plainly seen in so many places, that no one who trusted in God has ever been brought to confusion.

The fourth means is this (and this will serve both to acquire distrust of self, as well as trust in God)—when any thing occurs to be done, or some struggle with self has to be met, and you desire to overcome yourself, before you propose or make any resolution, consider first your own weakness; then, full of self-distrust, turn to the Divine Power, Wisdom and Goodness, and in reliance upon these, commence the action or conflict with fearlessness. Armed with these weapons, and with prayer (of which I shall speak presently), go forth to battle and to action.

Unless you observe this order, though you may think you are acting in reliance upon God, you will find generally that you are mistaken. For presumption is so natural and common to man, and withal so subtle, that it secretly lurks under an imagined self-distrust, and the trust we fancy we place in God.

To escape, then, as far as possible, from presumption, and to work in the spirit of self-distrust and trust in God, the consideration of your own weakness must go before the consideration of God's power, and both should precede all your actions.

CHAPTER 4

How we may know whether we are acting with Self-distrust and Trust in God.

ONE who is presumptuous oftentimes imagines that he has gained this spirit of self-distrust and trust in God, when he has really nothing of the kind. You may learn this by the way he takes his falls.

If after a fall you give way to despondency and vexation, and despairingly complain that you can make no progress, such feelings evidently show that you have been trusting in yourself and not in God.

And if your sadness and discouragement is much, then, there can be no doubt, that your trust in self was much, and your trust in God but little. For he who much distrusts himself and trusts in God, when he falls, is not surprised at it, neither does he become sad, bitter, and desponding; because he knows his fall is owing to his own weakness, and the little trust he placed in God.

On the other hand, as he grows in self-distrust, so more and more does he humbly trust in God; and hating intensely his sin and the rebellious passions which caused his fall, and mourning over it with a deep, calm, and meek sorrow, because of the offence against God, he at once resumes his efforts, and pursues his enemies with new resolution and energy even to the death.

I wish that some persons—who think themselves spiritual—would well consider these things; who cannot, or will not, give themselves a moment's peace, when they have committed a fault. Such persons rush off to their spiritual father chiefly to relieve themselves of their anxiety and vexation, which arise from self-love more than from any thing else, although their first concern should be to be cleansed from the stain of their sins, and to be fortified against temptation by the most holy Sacrament.

CHAPTER 5

Of the mistake of many, who hold Timidity for a Virtue.

MANY persons fall into this error. These consider the fearfulness and restlessness which follow upon sin a virtuous feeling (for is accompanied by a certain dissatisfaction with one's self), and do not see that it springs from a secret pride and from presumption, which are based on self-trust and self-reliance. Thinking themselves to be something, they have placed too much trust in their own strength. Their fall has obliged them to make the discovery that they do not possess this strength, and thus they are cast down and are full of wonder, as if something extraordinary had happened; and they become timid, because that trust in themselves, upon which they had foolishly leant, had given way.

The humble man knows no such experience, for his sole trust is in God. He places no reliance on his own powers. When he falls into any fault he is indeed sorry, but he is neither disquieted nor surprised, for he knows, as the light of truth has clearly manifested to him, that the fall is the result of his own weakness and misery.

CHAPTER 6

Further advice as to obtaining this Distrust of Self and Trust in God.

INASMUCH as our whole strength for conquering our enemies principally depends upon distrust of self and trust in God, I would furnish you with further counsels, that through the help of God you may attain this grace.

Concerning distrust in self, it is above all important that you should know and be fully persuaded that not all gifts, whether natural or acquired, nor all graces freely given, nor the knowledge of all Scripture, nor long and habitual exercise in God's service, are sufficient to enable you to do His Will; unless in every good work which has to be done, in every temptation which has to be conquered, in every danger which has to be avoided, and in every cross which has to be borne according to His Will, our heart is uplifted and sustained by His especial assistance, and His mighty Hand is outstretched to help us.

Therefore we ought to bear this in mind throughout our whole life— every day, every hour, every moment; and never allow the thought that there are any grounds for confidence in ourselves.

But with reference to trust in God, consider that it is as easy for God to overthrow many enemies as to overthrow few, and as easy for Him to conquer enemies old and experienced as to conquer the weak and unskillful.

Therefore suppose a soul to be heavy laden with sins; to have committed all possible sins, and to be full beyond description of all deformities; let such a soul have made every effort, have resorted to every possible means and spiritual exercise in order to rise above sin and acquire virtues, and yet have failed in making the least progress; nay, on the contrary, have been borne more than ever towards evil; yet that soul ought still to trust in God, and never to lay aside its spiritual weapons and exercises, but to continue strenuously to face the foe; for no one loses in this battle but he who ceases to fight and to trust in God.

He never ceases to help His soldiers, although He sometimes suffers them to be wounded. Only fight, for all depends on this. There are remedies at hand for healing the wounds of those warriors who look to God and to His help with confidence; and, when they least expect it, they shall find their enemies dead.

CHAPTER 7

Of Spiritual Exercise; and first of the Exercise of the Understanding, which must be preserved from Ignorance and Curiosity.

DISTRUST of self and trust in God are very necessary in this conflict, yet are they not all that is required, for if we had only these weapons we should lose the victory and fall headlong into many evils. Therefore to these we should add a third weapon, which is spiritual exercise. Spiritual exercise relates principally to the understanding and to the will.

With regard to the understanding, we must be on our guard against two faults, which very commonly impair its action.

Ignorance is the first of these; it darkens the understanding, and obstructs the entrance of truth—its proper object. Therefore you must by exercise of the understanding render it clear and bright, so that you may be able to see and distinctly discern what you need for purifying your soul from its disorderly passions, and adorning it with holy virtues.

Light may be obtained in two ways.

The first and most important means is prayer. The Holy Ghost should be entreated to pour this light into our hearts, which He will not fail to do, if we are true with God, and really seek nothing else but the fulfillment of His holy Will, and entirely submit our own judgment to that of our spiritual fathers.

The second way is, to gain the habit of viewing all things seriously and faithfully, in order to see them as they really are according to the teaching of the Holy Spirit, whether they are good or evil, and not according to their outward appearance, as judged by our senses, or by the world.

And if things are duly considered from this point of view, we shall clearly see that all, which the world in its blindness and corruption, in so many and in such various ways, seeks after and is eager to gain, is empty and delusive; and that the honors and pleasures of earth are but vanity and vexation of spirit; that injury and reproach, inflicted by the world, produce true glory, and that tribulation is a source of contentment. We shall learn, that to pardon our enemies and to benefit them is greatness of mind, and forms in us a close resemblance to God; that to despise the world is a nobler course than to have possession of it; that to obey for the love of God those far beneath us, is more generous and great than to rule great princes; that a humble conception of ourselves is more precious than the highest intellectual attainments; and, that the victory over and mortification of a slight rising of one of the passions is more glorious than the conquest of many cities, than the overthrow of powerful and armed forces, than the working of miracles and the raising of the dead.

CHAPTER 8

Of the Hindrances to a right Discernment of Things, and of the course which we should take in order to Judge truly concerning them.

OUR failure in judging of the things above mentioned, and of others, must be traced to the precipitancy with which at the first blush we regard them either with love or hatred; and thus, the understanding is blinded and hindered from taking a dispassionate view of them. Therefore, that we may not be in this way deceived, we must keep our will as much as possible in suspense and free from all inordinate affections.

When any object, then, is presented to you, view it with your understanding, and give it mature consideration before you conceive a hatred for it and reject it, if it is contrary to your natural inclinations; or, before you are inspired with a love for it, if it is agreeable to your taste.

For when the understanding, unclouded by passion, acts freely and clearly, it is able to detect the truth and to penetrate into the evil which is hidden under a fair appearance, and into the good which is veiled by a semblance of evil. Whereas, if the will is first inclined to love or hate any thing, the understanding afterwards cannot exercise a sound judgment upon it; because the affection, intervening between the object and the mind, prevents a just view of the object; and the understanding, giving back to the will this false representation, excites the will afresh to a love or hatred more vehement than before, in spite of every rule and law of reason.

By this affection the understanding becomes more and more darkened; and this darkness causes the object to seem more than ever desirable, or hateful to the will.

Therefore, unless the rule which has been laid down be observed (which is of the utmost importance), those two faculties—so noble and so excellent—the intellect and the will, will be made to act and re-act upon one another in a miserable circle, each in turn misleading the other, darkness producing thicker darkness, and error deeper error.

Guard yourself with the greatest care against any irregular affection; whatsoever the object which is presented to you may be, first examine it and test it by the light of the understanding, that you may discover its true nature, and especially by the light of grace and prayer, and with the guidance of your spiritual father.

And I would advise you to observe this most carefully in any outward works which are holy and of good report, for in such we are in greater danger of illusion and indiscretion, because they appear so good in themselves.

Some circumstance of time, place, or degree, or some fault as to obedience, may ruin the whole, as has been the case with many who have incurred great peril through the performance of actions in themselves praiseworthy and most holy.

CHAPTER 9

Of another Thing from which the Understanding must be preserved in order to exercise a Right Judgment.

THE other danger against which the understanding must be on its guard is curiosity; because, when we suffer it to be filled with hurtful, idle, and frivolous thoughts, we destroy its power of apprehending that which closely relates to the true mortification of ourselves and to our perfection.

On this account, you must become as one dead to all earthly things which do not concern you, though they may be harmless in themselves.

Ever restrain your understanding as much as possible, and love to keep it low.

Let the news and the fashions of the world—whatever they may be, great or small—be to you as though they were not; and, should they come in your way, reject them and drive them from you. Even in your desire to know heavenly things, preserve a sober and humble spirit, caring only to know Christ Crucified, His Life, and His Death, and whatever He requires of you.

Keep other things far from you, and in this way you will become well-pleasing to God; for He loves and counts as dear to Him those who desire and seek from Him only such things as are conducive to the love of His Divine Goodness, and to the fulfillment of His Will.

Every other petition and inquiry springs from self-love, pride, and the deceit of the devil.

If you follow these counsels you will escape many snares; for when the wily serpent sees that the will of those who are aiming at a spiritual life is strong and resolute, he uses his endeavors to overthrow their understanding, that he may thus master both the one and the other.

His plan is to instill into their minds—especially if they have an acute and subtle intellect, and are likely to be puffed up with pride—lofty and curious ideas; so that, being taken up with the pleasure of investigating such subjects, in which they falsely imagine that they are delighting in God, they may neglect to cleanse their hearts, and to acquire self-knowledge and true mortification. Thus, falling into the snare of pride, they make an idol of their own intellect.

Hence, gradually and imperceptibly, they come to the conviction that they have no need of the guidance or instruction of others, accustomed as they have been, in all cases, to lean upon the idol of their own judgment.

Such a condition is a perilous one, and not easily cured, for pride of the understanding is far worse than pride of the will; for the pride of the will, when manifest to the understanding, may in time be easily remedied by obedience to rightful authority; but how or by whom shall he be cured, who persists in regarding his own opinion as better than any other man's? and how shall he submit to the judgment of others, when he regards it as inferior to his own?

The understanding is the eye of the soul, to which we must trust for discovering and healing the wound of the proud will; if then the eye be weak, or blind, or swelled with the same pride, who shall be able to work a cure? and if the light become darkness, and that whereby we measure our actions be at fault, what will become of the rest?

Then resist without loss of time this malignant form of pride, before it penetrates into your inmost parts. Curb the quickness of your intellect; readily yield to the opinion of others; appear as a fool for the love of God, and you shall be wiser than Solomon.

CHAPTER 10

Of the Exercise of the Will, and of the End to which all our Actions, both inward and outward, should be directed.

IN addition to this exercise which you must apply to the understanding, you must also discipline your will, so that it may not be left to follow its own desires, but be in all things conformed to the good pleasure of God.

And remember, that it is not enough that you should will and do those things which are most pleasing to God; but, beyond this, you must will and do them, as being moved by Him, and with the motive of simply pleasing Him.

In this, even more than in the matter we have been considering in the previous chapter, lies the struggle with our nature, which seeks itself and its own pleasure in all things, and most of all in good and spiritual things; in these nature delights itself, reveling in them, as it suspects no harm from such food.

As soon then as they are presented to us, we gaze longingly upon them, and crave for them; not because we are moved to do the Will of God and wish only to please Him, but from a desire for that satisfaction and rest which we experience when we will those things which God wills.

The more excellent the object is which we desire, the more liable we are to be deceived. Thus, even in the desire after God Himself, we are in danger of falling into the snares of self-love, by having an eye to our own interests and to the advantages which we expect from God, rather than to His Will, Whose pleasure it is that we should love, desire, and obey Him simply for the sake of His Glory.

I will now tell you how to avoid this delusion, which would hinder your progress in holiness; and how to get into the habit of willing and doing all things according to the guidance of the Spirit of God, and with the pure motive of honoring and serving Him only, Who should be the Beginning and End of all our thoughts and actions. When any thing presents itself as in accordance with the Will of God, do not bring yourself to will it, until you have first lifted up your thoughts to God, to ascertain whether it is His Will that you should will it, and whether you will it because He does, and with the view of pleasing Him Alone.

Then let your will—thus moved and drawn by His—be bent upon willing it, because He wills it, and with the sole object of pleasing and glorifying Him.

The same course must be pursued in refusing the things which are contrary to God's Will. Do not refuse them till you have first fixed the eye of the understanding upon His Divine Will, Who wills that you should refuse them for the sake of pleasing Him.

Know, however, that we little suspect how deceitful and crafty our nature is, which is ever secretly seeking self, for we are often led to imagine that our object and motive is to please God, when it is quite the reverse.

Thus it comes to pass, that when we choose or refuse any thing for our own interest, we fancy that we are choosing or refusing it in the hope of pleasing, or fear of displeasing God.

The true and inward remedy for this delusion is purity of heart, which consists in this (which is really the aim of all this spiritual combat), namely—the putting off the old man, and the putting on the new.

In order to be well prepared, seeing you are full of self, beware at the beginning of every action, lest there be any admixture of selfish motives, and free yourself as much as possible from them. Neither choose, nor do, nor refuse any thing, unless you feel yourself moved and drawn to that course by the pure and simple Will of God.

If you cannot always feel that you are actuated by this motive in your conduct, especially in the inward acts of the mind, or in short outward actions, you must rest satisfied that you virtually have it, from the habit of maintaining a pure intention of pleasing God Alone in all you do.

But in actions which occupy some space of time, it is well not to be content with kindling this motive in your heart at the commencement of the action, but also to be careful to renew it frequently whilst the action is going on, and thus to preserve it alive to the very end.

If you neglect to do this, you will be in danger of falling into a snare, which our natural self-love prepares—for it is always more inclined and ready to follow its own course than to yield to God—namely, that of changing unconsciously after a time the objects and aims which you had in view when you began the action.

The servant of God, unless he is alive to this danger, often commences a work with the sole object of pleasing his Lord; but by degrees, and almost imperceptibly, he begins to take such pleasure in the work itself, that, losing sight of the Divine Will, he turns aside and becomes attached to the satisfaction he experiences in doing it, and to the advantage or credit he gains from it.

Then, if God Himself place some hindrance in his way, and the work is impeded by sickness, accident, or some one's interference, presently he is troubled and vexed, and begins to murmur at this or at that, not to say, sometimes even against God Himself—too clear a proof that he was not wholly seeking the Will of God, and that the motive was rotten and corrupt at its core.

For every soul which moves as God moves it, and aims at pleasing Him only, does not wish for this more than for that; nor to have any thing unless God wills to give it, nor to have it except in the way and for the time He appoints: such a soul is equally contented, whether having or not having it. For in either case it obtains its purpose, and its wish is fulfilled, which was nothing else but the good pleasure of God.

Therefore keep yourself habitually recollected, and be diligent in directing all your actions to this perfect end.

And if sometimes you are moved to do good (according to the bent of your natural disposition), by fear of the pains of Hell or hope of the joys of Paradise, you may even through these motives look ultimately to the good pleasure and Will of God, Who delights not at your departure into Hell, but at your entrance into His Kingdom.

The dignity and power of this motive no man can fully comprehend; a single action—even the least and most insignificant—done with the view of pleasing God Alone, and of glorifying Him, is worth infinitely more (so to speak) than many actions in themselves of the greatest value and worth, but springing from other motives. Thus, a single penny given to a poor man, with the sole object of pleasing His Divine Majesty, is more acceptable in His Sight than the entire renunciation of all our possessions, however great they may be, from some other motive, even for the attainment of the Bliss of Heaven—an object not merely good, but one which is in the highest degree desirable.

This practice of doing every thing with the simple intention of pleasing God Alone, appears difficult at first, but becomes easy and delightful by use, and by frequently fixing our desires on God Himself, and by longing after Him with the warm affections of our hearts, as our only and highest Good—the One Who deserves that all beings should seek Him for Himself, and should serve and love Him above all things.

The more seriously and constantly we meditate upon the Infinite Excellence of God, the more fervent and frequent will these acts of the will become; and we shall easily acquire in this way the habit of performing every action out of love to that Lord, Who Alone is worthy of it.

Lastly, in order to gain this divine intention, I advise you to seek it from God by earnest prayer; and to meditate often upon the numberless blessings, which God, out of pure love, and with no benefit to Himself, has bestowed, and is still bestowing upon us.

CHAPTER 11

Of some Considerations which may induce the Will to seek in all things the Good Pleasure of God.

MOREOVER, to render the will more inclined to desire in all things the good pleasure and the glory of God, call oftentimes to mind, that in many ways He has first honored and loved you.

By Creation—making you out of nothing, after His likeness; and by making all other creatures for your use.

By Redemption—sending, not an angel, but His Only-begotten Son, to redeem you, not with the corruptible price of silver and gold, but with His own Precious Blood, and His most painful and ignominious Death.

Consider, too, that every hour, and every moment, He defends you from your enemies, fights for you by His grace, offers you continually in the Sacrament of the Altar His Dear Son to be your strength and nourishment; is not this a token of the inestimable love and regard which the Infinite God has for you? We cannot, on the one hand, conceive how much value so great a Lord sets on us poor creatures, in our baseness and misery; and, on the other, how much we are indebted to His High Majesty, Who has done so many and so great things for us.

For if earthly masters, when they are honored even by men of poor and lowly condition, feel bound to honor them in return, how should our vileness behave itself towards the Sovereign Ruler of the Universe, by Whom we are so dearly prized and loved!

And, in addition to what has been already mentioned, keep ever a lively remembrance, that the Divine Majesty is infinitely worthy to be honored and served simply for Himself, and for His own good pleasure.

CHAPTER 12

Of the many Wills which are in Man, and of the Warfare between them.

ALTHOUGH in this spiritual combat man has two wills—the will of the mind, which we call the reasonable and superior will; and the will of the senses, which we call the sensual and inferior will, and which sometimes bears the names of appetite, flesh, sense, and passion: yet, as it is through the reason we are men, we cannot be said to will any thing when the lower will desires it, unless the higher will is disposed also to consent to it.

And herein lies the whole spiritual struggle; the reasonable will stands midway between the Divine Will which is above it, and the lower will of the flesh which is below it, and is continually assailed by the one or the other; each seeking to attract it, to bring it into subjection, and to rule it.

Great is the toil and struggle at the outset, which beginners experience when they resolve to amend their wicked lives, and—renouncing the world and the flesh—to yield themselves up to the love and service of Jesus Christ. For the battery, which the higher will sustains from the Divine and sensual wills warring on both sides of it, is so sharp and violent, that it entails much suffering.

Those who are experienced in the ways of virtue or vice do not feel this, but pursue the course they have entered upon with less difficulty; the virtuous yielding readily their will to the Divine Will, the vicious yielding without resistance to the will of the flesh.

But let no one suppose it possible to form true Christian virtues, and to serve God as he ought, unless he is ready in good earnest to do violence to his own inclinations, and to endure the pain of giving up all the things which pleased him, both great and small, and to which he had clung with earthly affection.

For this reason few reach perfection; for when they have overcome their greater faults with much toil, they will not continue to do violence to themselves, by bearing the vexation and weariness which the resistance of the countless little wishes and little movements of the passions involves. Thus these insignificant enemies are permitted to have their own way, and so obtain complete mastery over their hearts. All those who, if they do not take what belongs to others, yet cling inordinately to that which is lawfully their own, are of this class. If they do not take unlawful measures for the sake of obtaining honors, yet they do not, as they should, shun them; but, on the contrary, they covet them, and even sometimes by various ways seek to gain them. If they keep the fasts of obligation, they do not mortify their appetite as to superfluities, nor as to the delicacies which they crave for. If they live chaste lives, yet they do not abstain from some indulgences which hinder much their union with God and their growth in the spiritual life, and which even to the holiest persons are dangerous, and are especially so to those who fear them least, and therefore should be avoided by all to the utmost of their power.

The result of this course is, that all other good works are done in a lukewarm spirit, are mixed up with much self-seeking and secret imperfections, and are accompanied by a certain self-esteem, and by a desire for the praise and appreciation of the world.

Such persons not only fail to advance in the way of salvation, but, by turning back, stand in danger of relapsing into their old sins; because they have no love for true virtue, and show little gratitude to the Lord Who rescued them from the bondage of the Devil. Moreover, they are too blind and ignorant to see their real danger, whilst they delude themselves with the idea that they are in a safe condition.

Here we discover a great error, and one so much the more injurious as it is the less guarded against. Many who aspire to the spiritual life, being rather lovers of themselves than of that which is needful (although indeed they know it not), select for the most part those practices which accord with their own taste, and neglect others which touch to the quick their natural inclinations and sensual appetites, to overcome which all reason demands that they should put forth their full strength.

Therefore, beloved, I advise and entreat you to cherish a love for that which is painful and difficult, for such things will bring you victory over self—on this all depends. That victory will be the more certain and speedy, the more resolutely you give your heart to those toils which in holiness and in war are the lot of beginners; and if you love the toil and hardship of the struggle, rather than the victory and the virtue, you shall the sooner gain all things.

CHAPTER 13

Of the way to resist the Sensual Impulses, and of the Acts to be performed by the Will, in order to acquire Habits of Virtue.

WHENEVER the reasonable will is attracted by the will of the flesh on one side, and by the Divine Will on the other, each contending for the mastery, it will be necessary to exercise yourself in many ways, in order that the Divine Will may in all things prevail within you.

First, whenever you are assaulted and buffeted by the impulses of the lower nature, you must resist them manfully, so that the higher will may not consent.

Secondly, when the assaults have ceased, excite them again, so as to have an opportunity of overcoming them with greater force and energy. Then challenge them again a third time, so as to accustom yourself to repulse them with scorn and horror. These two challenges to battle should be made in the case of every unruly appetite, with the exception of temptations of the flesh, of which we will treat in their place.

Lastly, you should make acts contrary to each evil passion you have to resist. You will understand this the better by the following example:

Suppose, then, you are attacked by feelings of impatience. Look well into yourself, and you will discover that the higher will is continually aimed at by these temptations, in order to incline it to consent to them.

At once resort to the first thing which has been recommended; use the higher will repeatedly in opposing these feelings, resist them with all your might, that you may not be drawn to consent to them.

Do not leave off the conflict till the enemy is, as it were, wearied out, dead, and yields himself vanquished.

But, beloved, see the malice of the Devil. When he perceives that we resolutely resist the rising of any passion, he not only refrains from stirring it, but when it is excited he seeks to quiet it for the time, lest, by the practice of resisting it, we should form the habit of the opposite virtue.

And besides this, he would dexterously lead us to believe, that we have as brave soldiers quickly trampled under foot our enemies at one blow, so that he may entrap us with the snares of pride and vainglory.

Therefore, pass on from a first to a second encounter, by recalling to memory and exciting anew within you those thoughts which led to the temptation of impatience, until you are conscious of the feeling again; then resist with a stronger will than before, and with greater force repress the feelings.

And because, unless we thoroughly hate them, we are still in danger of being overcome by fresh attacks from our enemies—however successful we may have been in resisting them from a sense of duty and a desire to please God—you must face them a third time, and drive them far from you, not only with dislike but with disdain, picturing them to yourself as worthy of hatred and abhorrence.

Lastly, in order that the soul may be adorned and perfected with habits of virtue, you must often make inward acts which shall be directly opposed to your unruly passions.

Thus, if you want to gain perfect patience, when you have received an affront which temps to impatience, it will not be enough to exercise yourself in the three ways of fighting which I have already described, you must learn further to desire and love the slight you have received, wishing for a repetition of it, and from the same person; awaiting and disposing yourself to suffer still greater insults. These contrary acts are necessary for our perfection in holiness, because the above-named exercises of resistance—many and efficacious as they are—are not sufficient to pluck out the roots of sin.

And therefore (to continue the same instance) although, on receiving an insult we may not consent to the feelings of impatience, but fight against them in the three ways which have been recommended; yet, unless we accustom ourselves by many and constant acts of the will to love contempt and rejoice in it, we shall never be free from the vice of impatience, springing as it does from a regard for our own reputation and a dread of contempt.

And if the root of this sin be left alive, it will be sure to spring up afresh again and again, until virtue is weakened, and wholly choked by it; it will keep us in continual danger of a relapse upon every occasion. Therefore, without these contrary acts, the true habit of virtues can never be acquired.

And keep in mind also, that these acts must be so frequently made, as to be sufficient to destroy the sinful habit; for this habit, having been formed by repeated acts of sin, can only be removed by repeated acts of the opposite virtue, and thus a counter-habit of holiness be attained.

Moreover, a greater number of good acts are required to form a habit of virtue than of evil acts to form a vicious habit; in that the former are not in alliance with our nature, which is corrupt, but the latter are always aided by it.

Again, I would add to all that has been said, that, if the virtue you are striving to acquire need it, you must perform the outward acts in conformity with the inward; as, for example, speaking gently and lovingly, and, if possible, rendering services, to those who have in any way vexed and thwarted you.

And although these acts—both inward and outward—are done, or seem to be done, with such weakness of spirit as to make them appear to be a most unwilling service, yet you must on no account fail to do them; because, however weak they may be, they will keep you strong and secure in the battle, and make easy before you the path to victory.

Stand on your guard, and be self-controlled, so as to be ready to resist every assault of the passions, not only such as are hot and violent, but also the slightest and the gentlest movement; for these latter open the way for the former, and thus habits of sin are afterwards generated in us.

It comes to pass, from the little care men take to root out of their hearts lesser desires, that, after having conquered the stronger cravings of the same passion, many, when they least expect it, have been assaulted and vanquished by their old enemies more completely and fatally than at first.

Be mindful, too, sometimes to mortify and check yourself in things which are lawful but not necessary; for, from such a course of discipline, many good results will follow.

You will in this way dispose yourself more and more for victory over self in other things, you will gain strength and skill to struggle against temptations, you will avoid manifold devices of the Devil, and perform a work very pleasing to the Lord.

Beloved, I speak plainly to you; if, in the way which I have taught you, you will go on faithfully and constantly in these holy exercises for reforming and mastering yourself, then, I promise you, that you shall in a short time make much progress, and become really spiritual, and not in name only.

But in no other way, or course of discipline—however such may commend itself to you and be agreeable to your taste, yea, though it may seem to unite you in secret converse with your Lord—can I assure you that you will attain any real virtue or holiness. For this does not consist in (as I told you in the first chapter)—neither does it spring from—exercises which are pleasant to us and which accord with our natural tastes, but it is the fruit of the crucifying of the flesh with all its actions, and the renewing of man by the practice of the virtues of the Gospel, and the uniting him to his Crucified Creator.

Depend upon it, that as habits of sin are produced by many and repeated acts of the higher will, yielding itself to the sensual appetite; so, on the other hand, habits of the virtues of the Gospel are acquired by the performance of frequent and repeated acts of conformity to the Divine Will, as it calls us to the practice of different virtues from time to time.

For as our will can never become vicious or earthly, however fiercely assaulted or allured by the lower nature, unless it inclines towards or consents to the temptations; so, on the other hand, our will, however forcibly drawn and assailed by inspirations and Divine grace, will never become virtuous or be united to God, so long as by inward, and it may be, outward acts, it does not suffer itself to be brought into conformity with His Will.

CHAPTER 14

What ought to be done when the higher Will seems to be wholly overcome and stifled by the lower Will, and by its Enemies.

IF sometimes the higher will should seem to you powerless against the lower, and its other enemies, because you do not feel that your will is effectually set against them, yet stand firm and do not leave off fighting; for you must regard yourself as victorious, until you can clearly see that you have given way.

For since the higher will can act without the lower, so the higher can never be compelled by the lower to yield, however hot the assaults of the latter may be.

God has, in truth, given to the will such liberty and such power, that, if all the senses, all evil spirits, and all the world were to conspire together, and with their combined strength to assault and oppress it, the will could still in spite of them will or will not whatever it liked with perfect freedom, and could assert itself when it liked, and as often as, for as long as, in what manner, and for whatever end, best pleased it.

And if these enemies should ever attack you and press you with such violence as almost to stifle your will, so as to leave you, as it were, no breath to make an act of the will against them; yet do not lose courage, nor throw down your arms, but in such a case make use of your tongue and defend yourself by saying—"I do not yield to you, I do not consent to you"; after the manner of one who has been grasped and thrown to the ground by an enemy leaping upon him, and, when he is unable to thrust at him with the point of his sword, contrives to strike him with the hilt.

And as he strives to spring backwards so as to wound his enemy with the point of the sword, so do you retire into the consideration of yourself, the knowledge that you are nothing, and that you can do nothing. Then, putting your trust in God Who can do all things, strike a blow at the passion which attacks you, and say—"Help me, O Lord; help me, my God; help me, Jesus, Mary's Son, that I may not yield to this."

You may also, if the enemy gives you time for it, call in your understanding to aid your will, and by the use of various considerations impart to the will fresh power and spirit against the enemy. Thus, for example, when you are in some persecution or trouble, and are so attacked by temptations to impatience that the will cannot, or at least will not, stand up against them, you will proceed to encourage it by considering some points, such as the following:

First, consider, that if you have brought upon yourself the evil under which you are suffering, you deserve to bear it; for, in such a case, every rule of justice requires you to bear patiently the punishment which you have yourself been the means of inflicting.

Secondly, if you are not to blame in this particular matter, think that there are many faults which you have committed, for which you have received no chastisement from God, nor have you punished yourself for them as you ought. And seeing that the Divine mercy has changed the punishment of these faults, which should have been eternal, or at least should last for ages in another world, into this light affliction, ought you not to receive it willingly, or even thankfully?

Thirdly, if the thought should come that the penance is a long one in comparison with the offence against the Divine Majesty—a thought which no one can ever lawfully indulge—you must remember, that it is only through the strait gate of much tribulation that any can enter into the Kingdom of Heaven.

Fourthly, think that were it possible to enter by an easier way, the law of love would not allow you to dream of doing so, seeing that the Son of God, with all His friends and His members, reached that Kingdom by the road of thorns and crosses.

Fifthly, the chief thought upon which your mind should dwell in this, and in all other temptations, is the Will of your God, Who, for the love He has for you, takes unspeakable delight in every act of holiness and mortification which you, as His faithful and devoted soldier, perform in return for His love to you. And be thoroughly convinced of this, that the more unreasonable in itself the trouble is, and the more shameful on account of the person from whom it comes and therefore to you the more vexatious and difficult to be borne, so much the more pleasing will you be to the Lord, if, in things disordered in themselves and especially grievous to you, you can approve and love His Divine Will and Providence, by which every event—however irregular it may seem to be—is disposed after a most perfect rule and order.

CHAPTER 15

Some Suggestions about the manner of Fighting; and especially against what Enemies, and with what Virtues, we should contend.

YOU have seen already, how you must fight if you would conquer self, and adorn yourself with virtues.

Know, also, that to gain a quicker and easier conquest over your enemies, it is expedient, nay, necessary, that the conflict should be carried on daily, and especially the conflict with self-love; learn to receive, therefore, as dear friends, all the slights and insults which the world can heap upon you.

From our want of attention to this strife, and from making it of too little account, it frequently happens, as I have said before, that our victories are few and imperfect, are hardly won, and are not lasting.

Further, I warn you that you must fight with great steadfastness of purpose. And this gift you will easily gain, if you seek it by prayer; and if, when on the one hand you take into account the endless hatred and rage of your enemies, and the vast number of their squadrons and armies: you, on the other hand, consider how infinitely greater is the Goodness of God, and the love with which He loves you, and how much mightier too are the Angels of Heaven, and the prayers of the Saints, who are fighting on our side.

Animated by these reflections, how many, many poor weak women have resisted and overcome all the power and wisdom of the world, all the assaults of the flesh, and all the fury of Hell!

Therefore, you need never be disheartened, though at times the assaults of your enemy seem perpetually renewed, and though they threaten to last all your lifetime, and though certain falls on every side menace you; for, remember—besides what has been already said—that the whole strength and wisdom of our enemies is in the Hands of our Divine Captain, for Whose honor we contend.

He values us inexpressibly; and having Himself called us and commanded us to engage in the battle, not only will He never suffer you, as far as He is concerned, to be overcome, but He Himself will fight for you, and give your enemies into your hand, in His own good time; and this to your greater reward, though He keep you waiting even to the last day of your life.

All you have to do is to fight valiantly, and never to throw down your arms, nor flee, however many wounds you may have sustained.

Finally, to spur yourself on to fight courageously, you must bear in mind that from this conflict there is no escape; for not to fight is all one with being taken prisoner or slain. Besides, the fury and bitter hatred of our enemies are such, that there is no possibility of any truce or peace.

CHAPTER 16

In what way the Soldier of Christ should take the Field early in the Morning.

AS soon as you wake, the first thing to be observed by the eyes of your mind, is your position in the field of battle, where you are hemmed in by enemies, and under the absolute necessity of fighting, or perishing for ever.

Within this view represent to yourself, your enemy—the evil inclination which you have sworn to renounce, facing you on the one side, and armed so as to be able to wound and kill you; and, on the right hand, see your victorious Leader, Jesus Christ, with His most holy Mother, the Virgin Mary, and her beloved husband, Joseph, and countless hosts of Angels and Saints, especially St. Michael the Archangel; on the left hand, behold the Devil from beneath, with his followers, ready to kindle the passion in question, and to entice you to yield to it.

Then you shall seem to hear a voice, as of your guardian Angel, saying unto you, "You have today to fight against this enemy and against others too. Let not your heart sink, and do not lose courage; nor yield from fear or on any other account, for our Lord, your Captain, stands beside you, with all His glorious hosts with Him; and He will fight for you against all your enemies, and will not permit them to prevail against you either by force or oppression.

"Only stand firm, and do violence to yourself, and do not shrink from the pain which such a discipline will cost you. Cry unceasingly from the depths of your heart, and call upon the Lord, asking also for the help of the Blessed Virgin and all the Saints, and then you will be certain to gain the victory. If you are weak and inexperienced in the strife, and your enemies appear to be many and powerful, yet much more is the strength which He, Who made and redeemed you, will give you than that which they possess; and beyond all measure and comparison is your God mightier than they, and His Will for your salvation stronger than the will of your enemies for your destruction.

"Fight therefore, and do not spare yourself the pain; for from the toil in overcoming and doing violence to your evil inclinations, and from the suffering which the war against sinful habits necessitates, you shall gain the victory, and win the exceeding great reward, and therewith purchase for yourself the Kingdom of Heaven, and the everlasting union of your soul with God."

Begin the conflict in the Name of the Lord, taking up the armor of distrust of self and trust in God, with prayer and spiritual exercises; with these arms challenge this foe, that is, this inclination, whatever it may be, which, according to the order above laid down, you have resolved to overcome. Do this, now by open resistance, now by deep loathing, or again, by acts of the opposite virtue; wounding it with oft-repeated and deadly blows, in order to please your Lord, Who, with His whole Church Triumphant, is looking on and watching the combat.

I tell you again, that you must not grow weary in the conflict, but must ever bear in mind that it is the bounden duty of all to serve and please God; that the necessity of fighting is absolute, and escape impossible without wounds or death. I tell you, also, that if, as a deserter you were to fly from God, and give yourself to the delights of the world and of the flesh, you would still, in spite of yourself, be forced to labor in the sweat of your brow against many and many a contradiction which would pierce your heart with deadly anguish.

Consider, then, what madness it would be to incur all this toil and pain—which only lead to greater toil and pain with endless death—simply to avoid that which will soon be over, and which would bring us to a life eternal and infinitely blessed in the everlasting enjoyment of our God.

CHAPTER 17

Of the Order to be observed in the Conflict with our Evil Passions.

IT is of the utmost importance that we should know what order to observe in this combat, lest—as is the case with too many, to their great loss—we fight in a casual or formal manner. The best order for proceeding in this battle against your enemies and your evil inclinations is as follows:

Having diligently examined your heart, and searched into the different thoughts and affections which encompass it, and having discovered by what passion it is most of all possessed and governed; then against this first, direct your attack. If it happens that, meanwhile, you are assailed by other enemies, you must turn against the one which at the moment threatens you and most closely attacks you, and then return at once to the chief point of conflict.

CHAPTER 18

Of the way to overcome Sudden Risings of the Passions.

IF you have not gained the habit of warding off sudden attacks, whether of injuries or adverse occurrences; in order to acquire it, your plan will be to anticipate such attacks, and desire to bear them over and over again, and thus dispose yourself for actually receiving them.

The way to forestall them is this—having considered the bent of your passions, consider also the places where, and the persons with whom, you are likely to be thrown; you may easily thus conjecture what may probably happen.

And should any other vexatious circumstance arise, which you had not foreseen, in addition to the general help which a prepared mind gives, even to meet evils beyond those for which it was prepared, you may with advantage avail yourself of the following mode of meeting it:

As soon as you first feel the blow of this unexpected injury or trial, be on your guard at once, and make the effort to lift up your mind to God, contemplating His unspeakable goodness and love to you, in sending you this trial in order that you, bearing it out of love for Him, may be the more purified, and may be brought near and united to Him.

And, realizing how greatly it pleases Him that you should suffer this, turn to yourself and say, "Ah, why so reluctant to bear this cross, which is laid upon you not by this or that person, but by your Father in Heaven?" Then turn to the cross, embrace it with the fullest resignation and joy, and say, "O cross, formed by Divine Providence before I was born! O cross, sweetened for me by the sweet love of my Crucified One—nail me now to thee, that I may give myself to Him Who, dying upon thee, hath redeemed me!"

And if, at the onset, the passion so prevail over you, that you cannot lift up your heart to God, but remain wounded, strive even then to do as at the beginning, and to fight as if you had not received a wound.

The most effectual remedy, however, against these sudden impulses, is to cut out without delay the cause from which they spring.

Thus, if you find out that your affection for any thing is so great, that, whenever it is presented to you, you fall into a sudden agitation of mind, the best precaution for the future lies in the habitual effort to uproot the affection.

But if the agitation is caused not by a thing, but by a person, for whom you have such an aversion that every little action annoys and irritates you, the remedy then is, to force yourself to incline your will to love him and to regard him, not only because he is a creature like yourself, formed by the Almighty Hand, and formed anew by the same Divine Blood, but also, because he affords you an opportunity, if you will accept it, of becoming like unto your Lord, Who was loving and kind unto all.

CHAPTER 19

How to resist the Lusts of the Flesh.

THIS temptation must be dealt with in a way peculiar to itself, and unlike any other. In order, therefore, to fight successfully against it, three periods of time must be observed:

1. Before the temptation.
2. During the temptation.
3. After the temptation.

1. Before the temptation, the struggle must be against the things which lead to it.

First, you must not war against this vice by confronting it, but, on the contrary, by fleeing with all your might from the thing or person that may have the least likelihood of exciting it.

And if through necessity you have to converse with such a person, be as brief as you can, and preserve a grave and modest demeanor, and let your words incline to harshness, rather than to excess of tenderness and affability.

Presume not on your own strength, if you are free, and have been for very many years free, from the temptations of the flesh; for this cursed vice does in an hour what for years it has failed to do, often making its advances stealthily; and the more it comes in the garb of a friend without exciting suspicion, the more grievous are the injuries and the more fatal the wounds it inflicts.

And often there is more to be feared—as experience has often shown, and shows every day—where intercourse seems perfectly legitimate, as with relations, or in the discharge of duties, or with persons who from their virtues ought to be beloved. For with this too frequent and unguarded intercourse, the poisonous pleasure of sense insinuates itself; gradually instilling itself, until it penetrates into the very depths of the soul, and darkens the reason more and more, until things which are most dangerous are regarded as of no account; such as loving looks, words of mutual endearment, and charms of conversation; and thus, step by step, a ruinous fall approached, or at the least some painful temptation which is with great difficulty overcome.

Once more I say to you—fly! for you are as tow. Trust not to being moistened, as it were, with the water of a good and strong purpose, and a resolution rather to die than to offend God; for by frequent excitement, the heat of the fire will gradually dry up the water of your good purpose, and, when you least expect it, will so attack you, that no respect will be left for friends or kindred, no fear of God, no regard for life or reputation, nor for all the pains of Hell. Therefore fly! fly! if indeed you would avoid being overtaken, made prisoner, and slain.

Secondly, avoid idleness, and be watchful and active, engaged with the thoughts and deeds suitable to your state of life.

Thirdly, never rebel against the will of superiors, but obey readily, doing promptly all that they bid you; and the more willingly obey those who humble you, and who are most opposed to your natural will and temperament.

Fourthly, beware of rashly judging your neighbor, and especially in regard to this sin; and if his fall be evident, show him pity rather than indignation, and do not despise him; try rather to gather from his fall the fruits of lowliness and self-knowledge, acknowledging yourself to be dust and nothing; draw near to God in prayer, and avoid more carefully than ever any intercourse, which may bring with it even the shadow of danger.

For if you are ready to judge and despise another, God will correct you to your cost, and will permit you to fall into the same fault, that you may be convinced of your pride; that, by such a humiliation, you may at the same time find the remedy for both these sins.

And, even if you do not fall into this sin, remember, that, unless you put away this sin of rash judgment, your state will still be one to be much concerned about.

Fifthly and lastly, take heed, lest, when you are favored with some spiritual sweetness and delight, you fall into the snare of a certain vain complacency, and imagine yourself to be something, and that your enemies are no longer able to attack you, because you entertain towards them such a feeling of disgust, hatred, and loathing. If you are put off your guard in this manner, you will easily fall.

2. During the time of temptation, find out whether it arises from inward or outward causes.

By outward, I mean such things as curiosity of the eyes and ears, indulgence in fine dress, habits, and conversations which stir up this vice.

The remedies in such cases are modesty and decency, guard of the eyes and ears from what may stir up this evil, and (as I have said already) flight.

The inward causes are, either vigor of body, or imaginations of the mind which proceed either from our evil habits, or from the suggestions of the Devil.

The vigor of body must be brought down by fasting, chastisement, mortification, watchings, and similar hard measures; but these must be undertaken with discretion and under obedience.

Unholy thoughts, from whatever source they arise, must be remedied as follows:

First, by constant occupation in the different duties which are consistent with our state of life; secondly, by prayer, and by meditation.

Let prayer be made in the following way:

When you are first slightly conscious, I do not say of the evil thoughts themselves, but of those which lead up to them, at once fly in spirit to your Crucified Lord, and say, "My Jesus! my dear Jesus! make haste to help me, lest I fall into the enemy's hands!" At other times, clasping the Cross on which your Lord hangs, and kissing again and again the Wounds of His Sacred Feet, say lovingly—"O beautiful Wounds, chaste Wounds, holy Wounds, wound now my heart, miserable and impure as it is, and free it from all that is offensive in Thy Sight."

At the time of the temptation to carnal indulgences I do not recommend you to meditate upon certain points—as many books suggest—as a remedy against this temptation; such, for instance, as the vileness of this vice, its insatiableness, the loathing and remorse which follow upon it, the peril and loss of goods, life, honor, and all such things. For this is so far from being a sovereign remedy against such temptations, that it may prove hurtful rather than otherwise; for if, on the one hand, the mind dispels these thoughts, on the other, it affords the opportunity and exposes us to the danger of taking pleasure in them, and consenting to the delight. Therefore the sure remedy is flight in all these cases, both from the thoughts themselves, and from every thing—however contrary to them—which may bring them to the mind again.

Take, therefore, for your subject of meditation the Life and Passion of our Crucified Redeemer for this purpose. And if, during your meditation, the images of the same thoughts come before the mind's eye against your will, and molest you more than ever—as is frequently the case—do not therefore despond, nor leave off your meditation, neither turn your attention to these thoughts with a view to resisting them, but pursue it with all possible intenseness, taking notice of these thoughts, which in no sense belong to you. There is no better plan of resisting them than this, however frequently these assaults may come.

You may finish your meditation with this, or some similar request— "Deliver me, O my Creator and Redeemer, from my enemies, to the honor of Thy Passion and of Thy unspeakable Goodness"; and then give no further thought to the sin, for the bare remembrance of it is not without danger.

Never, at any time, stay to dispute with such temptations, whether you have consented or not; for this is a device of the Devil, who seeks, under the guise of a good motive, to harass you and render you distrustful and despondent; or hopes, by keeping your attention on such questions, to plunge you into some wrong pleasure.

Therefore, in this temptation (when you are not clear as to whether you have consented or not) it will be sufficient to confess the whole as briefly as possible to your spiritual father, and then to rest satisfied with his opinion upon the matter, without thinking about it more. Be careful, however, that you lay bare before him every thought, and do not let human respect or shame hinder you from doing so.

For if in all cases we need the virtue of humility in order to overcome our enemies, we must exercise it in this more than in any other; this vice being, as a rule, the punishment of pride.

3. When the temptation has gone, you must act in this way: However free, and however secure you fancy yourself to be from all danger, yet keep your mind far away from those subjects which may have occasioned the temptation, even should you feel an inducement to do otherwise for the sake of some good and virtuous end. For this is a device of our corrupt nature, and a snare of our subtle enemy, who transforms himself into an angel of light, that he may draw us into the darkness.

CHAPTER 20

Of the Way to overcome Sloth.

THAT you may not fall into the miserable bondage of sloth, which not only hinders all spiritual progress, but also delivers you into the hands of your enemies, you must avoid all curiosity and earthly attachment, and every occupation which does not belong to your state of life.

You must then exert yourself to obey every good inspiration from above, and every command of those who are over you; doing every thing at the time and in the manner which they approve of.

Never delay, even for an instant; for that first indulgence will bring another in its train, and then a third, and then others after it; and finally the senses will yield more easily than at the beginning, being already allured and captivated by the pleasure which they have tasted. The consequence of this is, that, when it is too late we begin to act, or neglect altogether a duty which is then too irksome.

Thus gradually the habit of sloth is formed, which in time so grows upon us, and brings us into such a state, that at the very instant, when we are bound hand and foot with the chains of sloth, we vainly purpose to be more diligent and more active at another time, being obliged with blushes to own to ourselves our present excessive indolence.

This sloth runs through every thing we do, and not only infects the will, by making it hate work, but also blinds the understanding, so that it cannot detect how vain and unfounded are its purposes of doing diligently and promptly, at some future day, that which should be done at once, but which is either voluntarily left undone, or deferred to some other time.

And it is not enough to do at once what you have to do: we must, in order to do it as perfectly as possible, do it at the very time which the nature and quality of the work demand, and with all the diligence which befits it.

For that is not diligence, but a very subtle form of sloth, which leads us to do our work before its time, and to dispatch it hastily, not caring whether it be done well or not, so that we may then quietly give ourselves up to the enjoyment of a sluggish rest, upon which our thoughts were bent, when we were hurrying through our task.

This great evil proceeds from the want of duly considering the value of a good work, when done at the right time, and with a determination to overcome the toil and difficulty which the sin of sloth puts in the way of newly-enlisted soldiers.

You must often, therefore, call to mind, that one ejaculation to God, one single bending of the knee to His honor, is worth more than all the treasures of the world; and that, whenever we do violence to ourselves and to our bad inclinations, the Angels bring to our souls a crown of glorious victory from the Heavenly Kingdom. And consider also, on the other hand, that from the slothful, God by little and little withdraws the graces which He had bestowed upon them; whilst to the diligent He gives more abundant graces, and permits them at last to enter into His joy.

As to the toil and hardship, if you feel at first unable boldly to face it, hide them from you, that they may not seem so formidable as sloth would represent them.

The work you have before you, perhaps, is to gain some virtue by many repeated acts of it, and with many days' toil; and the enemies you have to encounter seem numerous and powerful. Begin, then, these acts, as if you had but few to make, and but a short time to endure the conflict. Fight against one enemy at a time, as if there were no more to be resisted; and fight with full confidence that, with the help of God, you will be stronger than all who are against you. By this means sloth will gradually lose ground, and give place by degrees to the entrance of the opposite virtue.

The same plan holds good in prayer. If one hour is allotted for prayer, and to sloth the length of the time appears difficult, enter upon it with the intention of spending ten minutes; then, when that time has passed, take ten minutes more; and so you will pass easily through the remainder, until the whole hour is spent. But if, after ten or twenty minutes, you feel a violent distaste and difficulty in going on, leave off for a time, lest you become weary; but return again after a little while to the exercise you had quitted.

You should adopt the same course in regard to manual labor, when it is your duty to undertake works which seem to sloth interminable and tedious, and which, therefore, you cannot view without vexation of mind; begin, nevertheless, courageously and calmly with one, as if it were the only one you had to do; and when, having confined your attention to that, you have finished it, then go on with the next; and in this way, you will get through the whole of them with far less exertion than your slothfulness could have conceived to be possible.

But if you do not follow this plan, and face with courage the toil and hardship which lie in your way, the vice of sloth will so gain the mastery over you, that you will be always harassed and vexed, not only by the present toil and struggle, which ever accompany the first practice of virtue, but also by the sight of that which is afar off. You will live in dread of being tried and assailed by enemies, or of seeing some one impose a fresh burden on your shoulders; so that, even in times of peace, you will be full of apprehension.

Further, remember, beloved, that this vice of sloth, with its secret poison, will not only gradually kill the early and tender roots which would ultimately have produced habits of virtue, but also habits of virtue which are already formed. It will, like the worm in the wood, insensibly eat away and destroy the very marrow of the spiritual life. It is by this means the

Devil spreads his nets and traps in the way of all of us, but especially of those who seek to become spiritual.

Watch, therefore, with prayer, and labor with diligence, and delay not to weave the web of your wedding-garment, for you should be found clothed in it when the Bridegroom comes.

Remember every day, that He Who gives you the morning does not promise the evening, and when He gives you the evening, does not promise the next morning.

Spend, then, every moment of the passing hour in a way which is pleasing to God, as if it were your last, and so much the more carefully, seeing that for every moment you must give the strictest account.

Finally, I advise you to consider that day as lost, in which (though you may have transacted much business in it) you have neither gained a victory over some sinful inclination, or form of self-will, nor thanked the Lord for all His benefits, and above all for His Sorrowful Passion endured for you, and for His Fatherly and sweet chastisements, when He has made you worthy to receive from Him the inestimable treasure of some trial.

CHAPTER 21

Of the Guard of the Outward Senses, and how from these we may pass to the Contemplation of the Divinity.

GREAT care and constant practice are necessary for the right control and guard of our outward senses. For the appetite, which may be regarded as the captain of our corrupt nature, is madly bent upon seeking pleasures and satisfaction; and, being incapable of itself of obtaining them, it makes use of the senses as its soldiers, and as natural instruments for laying hold of their objects, the images of which it takes, appropriates, and impresses on the mind. From this a sensation of pleasure arises, which, by means of the close connection between the soul and the flesh, spreads itself through all the sensual part of our nature, and thus soul and body are possessed by a common contagion, which corrupts the whole.

You see the evil; now mark the remedy.

Be careful not to let your senses wander as they like; nor to employ them merely for the sake of pleasure, without any good end, or without having in view either usefulness or necessity. And if, through want of watchfulness, they have already wandered too far, recall them at once, or restrain them, so that instead of remaining in a state of miserable bondage to vain pleasures, they may gather a noble spoil from each object, and bring it home to the soul; and that the soul, by an act of recollection, may spread her wings with renewed energy towards Heaven, and rise to the contemplation of God. This may be thus done:

When an object is presented to any one of your outward senses, separate in thought the spirit and the material substance, and reflect that of itself it possesses none of those qualities which your senses attribute to it, but that all is the work of God, Who by His Invisible Spirit endows it with the being, beauty, goodness, or charm whatever it be which belongs to it. Then rejoice that your Lord Alone is the Cause and Principle of such great and varied perfections, and that in Himself they are all contained in the highest degree; for they are but the faintest shadows of His Infinite Excellence.

Whenever you discover yourself to be absorbed in the act of admiring some noble object, let your thoughts bring the creature down to its own nothingness, and let your mind's eye gaze upon the great Creator therein present, Who made it to be what it is; and, delighting in Him only, say—"O Divine Essence, above all things to be desired, what joy it is to think that Thou Alone art the Infinite Principle of every created being."

In the same way, when you behold the trees, the plants, and things of that kind, you will perceive that their life does not flow from themselves, but from the Invisible Spirit, Which Alone gives them life. Then you can say—"Behold here the true Life, from Whom, in Whom, and through Whom all things live and grow! O living satisfaction of this heart of mine!"

So, when you see any of the brute creation, you will lift up your thoughts to God, Who gives them sensation and powers of movement, saying—"O Thou First Mover, Who, moving all things, art Thyself unmoved by any, how do I exult in Thy stability and firmness!"

And when you rejoice in the beauty of some creature, separate that which you see from the Spirit Which you do not see, and consider, that all which appears outwardly fair, springs only from the Invisible Spirit, from Whom this outward beauty has its source, and say with all delight—"Behold these rivulets from the uncreated Fountain! behold these are little drops from the boundless Ocean of all good! Oh, how do I rejoice from my inmost heart at the thought of that Eternal, Infinite Beauty, Which is the Origin and Cause of all created beauty."

And when you behold in others, goodness, wisdom, justice, or other virtues, make the same separation in your mind, and say to your God, "O most rich Treasury of all virtues, how greatly do I rejoice, that from Thee Alone, and through Thee, flows every good; and that all in comparison of Thy perfection is as nothing! I thank Thee, Lord, for this and for all other good gifts, which Thou hast bestowed upon my neighbor; remember, Lord, my poverty and sore need of this very virtue!"

When you exert yourself to do any thing, bear in mind that God is the first Cause of this action, and that you are nothing but His living instrument; and, lifting up your thoughts to Him, say thus—"How great, O Sovereign Lord of all, is my inward joy, that without Thee I can do nothing, and that Thou art the first and chief Worker in all things."

If you eat or drink, think that it is God Who makes your food pleasant to you; and, rejoicing in Him Alone, you will be able to say—"Be glad, O my soul, that as there is no true satisfaction but in God, so in Him Alone in every thing you can delight."

When your senses are gratified by some sweet odor, do not rest in the enjoyment itself, but let your thoughts pass on to your Lord, from Whom the delight comes; and, filled with inward joy at this contemplation, say—"Grant, O Lord, that as I rejoice because all sweetness comes from Thee, so may my soul, cleansed and delivered from all earthly gratifications, mount up to Thee, and be acceptable as a sweet savor poured forth in Thy Presence."

When you are delighted with the harmonies of music and singing, turn your heart to God, and say—"How do I rejoice, O my Lord and God, in Thy Infinite Perfections, which not only form a more than heavenly harmony within Thyself, but also unite in one marvelous concert the Angels in Heaven and all creatures."

CHAPTER 22

How the same Things may offer us opportunities of regulating our Senses by passing on to Meditation on the Incarnate Word in the Mysteries of His Life and Passion.

I HAVE already shown you the way to raise your minds from sensible objects to the contemplation of God. Now learn how to use sensible objects as reminders of the Incarnate Word, by reflecting on the most Holy Mysteries of His Life and Passion.

All things in the universe may serve to this end, if, as I said before, you first behold God in them as the Sole First Cause, Who has given them all their being, beauty, and excellence. Passing on from thence, consider how great and boundless is His Goodness, Who, being the Sole Source and Lord of all creation, was pleased to descend so low as to become man, to suffer and die for man, thus permitting the very works of His Hands to arm themselves against Him and crucify Him.

Many objects, then, will bring particularly these Holy Mysteries before your mind's eye; such as weapons, cords, scourges, pillars, thorns, reeds, nails, hammers, and other instruments of His Passion.

The sight of a hovel may recall to our memory the stable and manger of our Lord. Rain may remind us of that rain of Divine Blood which watered the ground, falling from His Sacred Body in the Garden. Rocks will represent to us those which were split asunder at His Death; the earth will bring to remembrance the earthquake which then took place; the sun, the darkness which obscured it, and the sight of water will speak to us of that stream which flowed forth from His most Sacred Side. Other things may be used in a similar manner.

Whenever you taste wine, or other drink, think of the vinegar and gall which was given to your Lord.

If you enjoy a sweet perfume, think of the stench from the dead bodies which He smelt on Calvary.

Whilst dressing, have in mind how the Eternal Word clothed Himself with human flesh, that He might clothe you with His Divinity. When undressing, remember how the Savior was stripped of all His garments, in order to be scourged and nailed to the Cross for you.

If you hear the shouts and cries of a multitude, recall the hateful voices which shouted into His Divine ears, "Crucify Him! Crucify Him! Away with Him! Away with Him!"

When the clock strikes, remember the painful beating of the heart which Jesus endured in the Garden, as the fear of His approaching Death and Passion oppressed Him; or, imagine you are listening to the heavy blows by which they nailed Him to the Cross.

Whatever grief or pain you suffer yourself, or see others suffering, reflect that it is all nothing, when compared with the inconceivable anguish which pierced and wrung the Body and Soul of your Lord.

CHAPTER 23

Of other ways of Governing our Senses according to the different occasions which happen.

HAVING shown you how to raise your mind from outward things to the contemplation of the Divinity, and to the Mysteries of the Incarnate Word, I will here add some other helps for meditations in a different manner, that, as the tastes of our souls are various, so also may be the food which is supplied. Moreover, this may be useful not only to simple-minded persons, but also to those who are more talented and more advanced in the spiritual life, and who nevertheless are not always equally disposed or ready for more profound contemplations.

Nor need you fear that the suggestion of such a variety of methods will be perplexing, if you will only keep to the rule of discretion, and to the advice of others, which I would have you, not only in this instance but on all occasions, follow with lowliness and trustfulness.

When you look upon so many things of earth, which are pleasant to the eyes and valued, consider that they are utterly vile and as dung in respect of the Heavenly riches; after which, despising the whole world, aspire with your whole heart.

When you look towards the sun, consider how much brighter and more beautiful your soul is than it, if you are in the favor of the Creator; and if not in a state of grace, think that it is blacker and more abominable than the darkness of Hell.

When you raise your eyes to the heavens above you, let the eyes of your mind pierce through it to the Heaven of heavens, and there fix yourself in thought as in the place prepared for your eternal and most blessed resting-place, if you live innocently on earth.

If you hear the songs of birds, or other sweet strains, lift up your mind to the songs of Paradise, where sounds the endless Alleluia; and pray the Lord to make you meet to praise Him for ever, in union with those heavenly spirits.

If the beauty of a creature fascinates you, remember that the serpent of Hell lies hidden beneath it, anxious and ready to kill or at least wound you, and say to him—"Ah, accursed serpent, with what subtlety dost thou lay wait to devour me!" Then turn to God and say—"Blessed be Thou, my God, Who hast discovered to me the secret enemy, and rescued me from his ravenous jaws!" After this, fly at once from the allurement to the Wounds of your Crucified Lord, and let your mind be occupied with them, musing upon the great things your Lord suffered in His most Sacred Flesh in order to redeem you from your sins, and to render all carnal delights odious to you.

I would also remind you of another way of escape from this dangerous enticement, namely, to represent to yourself vividly how this object which so charms you, would appear in your eyes after death had worked its change.

When walking, think how each step brings you one nearer to death.

Let the birds in the air, and the water in the stream, remind you that your life even with greater swiftness is hurrying on to its close.

Let violent storms of wind, peals of thunder, and flashes of lightning bring you to the thought of the awful Day of Judgment; and on your bended knees worship God, and pray for grace and time to make due preparation for your appearing before His Supreme Majesty.

In the different accidents which may happen to you, you may act in the following manner:

When (for instance) you feel very melancholy and depressed in spirits, or are tried by heat or cold or any other bodily pain, lift up your heart to the Eternal Will, which has for your good and happiness appointed you this discomfort, and has arranged the time and duration of it. Then, rejoicing in this manifestation of the love of God, and for the opportunity of serving Him in the way which seems to Him best, say in your heart—"Behold in me the fulfillment of the Divine Will, which has from all eternity lovingly ordered that I should now undergo this trial. Blessed, ever-blessed, be my most gracious Lord!"

When any good thought arises in your heart, turn at once to God, and acknowledge that it comes from Him, and give thanks to Him for it.

When you read, seem to see beneath the words your Lord, and receive them as if at that moment they were proceeding out of His Divine Lips.

When you look on the Holy Cross, remember that it is the standard of your warfare; and, that if you forsake it, you will give yourself over into the hands of cruel enemies, but if you follow it, you will enter into Heaven, laden with glorious spoils.

When you see the sweet image of the Blessed Virgin, let your thoughts turn to her who reigns in Paradise, and be thankful that she was every moment ready to do the Will of God; that she bore, nourished, and tended the Redeemer of the world; and, that in our spiritual conflict, she is ever desirous to give us her sympathy and aid.

Let the images of Saints represent to you so many champions who, having bravely run their course, have opened the way by which, if you too run, you shall be crowned with them in endless glory.

When you see a church, you may, amongst other devout reflections, consider that your soul is the temple of God, and that you are therefore bound to strive to keep it pure and spotless, as His dwelling-place.

When you hear the three sounds for the Angelical Salutation, make the following short meditations on the words which are said before each of the little heavenly prayers. At the first stroke of the bell, give thanks to God for that message which came from Heaven to earth and was the beginning of our salvation. At the second, rejoice with the Blessed Virgin at the greatness to which she was raised through her most profound and matchless humility. At the third stroke, unite yourself with the most Blessed Mother and the Angel Gabriel in adoring the Divine Child newly conceived; and remember to bow your head with reverence at each stroke, and with a lower reverence at the last.

These meditations at the three strokes of the bell will serve for all seasons. The following for morning, noon, and night are more fitted for the season of the Passion; for we are especially bound to remember the sorrows endured by our Lady at that time, and should be open to the charge of ingratitude were we to neglect to do so.

In the evening, then, think of the anguish of that most pure Virgin, on account of the Bloody Sweat, the seizing in the Garden, and all the untold sorrows which through that night her Blessed Son endured.

In the morning, condole with her for what she suffered when her Son was brought before Pilate and Herod, was condemned to die, and when He came forth bearing His Cross.

At noon, pass on to the thought of the sword of grief which pierced the heart of this afflicted Mother at the Lord's Crucifixion and Death, and at that most cruel piercing of His most sacred Side.

These meditations on the grief of the Blessed Virgin will serve you from Thursday evening till Saturday at noon, the former will suit the other days of the week. I leave all this, however, to be settled by your own devotional attraction, and by the opportunities which external objects afford.

But to conclude in few words, I will only add—as a general rule for governing the senses—be watchful that, in all the occurrences of your life, whatever they may be, you are not moved or drawn, either by love or hatred of them, but only by the Will of God, embracing what God wills you to embrace, and hating what God wills you to hate.

And observe, that these different rules for governing the senses are not given to you that you should be always thinking about them; for your mind should be fixed on your Lord continually, Who wills that, by frequently making acts of the contrary virtues, and by resistance, you should conquer your enemies and subdue your evil passions. I have simply given you these directions to help you when you stand in need of them.

For you must know that there is little fruit in the multiplicity of spiritual practices, however excellent they may be in themselves. They often end in perplexity, self-love, instability, and the snares of the Devil.

CHAPTER 24

How to Rule the Tongue.

THE tongue of man needs to be well ruled and restrained, because we are all too inclined to let it run on and discourse upon things which are most agreeable to our senses.

It is usually pride which is at the root of much speaking. We persuade ourselves that we know a great deal, and take delight in our own conceits; and then, we strive by a multitude of words to convey to others the same idea, so as to gain an ascendancy over them, as though they stood in need of our instruction. To express in a few words all the evils which arise from much speaking is an impossibility.

Talkativeness is the mother of idleness, the evidence of ignorance and folly, the door of slander, the purveyor of falsehood, the damper of fervent devotion.

A multitude of words kindles the evil passions, and these in turn incite the tongue to continue its thoughtless utterances.

Indulge not in lengthy conversations with those who are bored thereby, lest you weary them, nor with those who like to listen to you, lest you go beyond the bounds of modesty.

Do not speak loudly, or in a dictatorial manner, which is odious to others and a mark of presumption and vanity.

Never speak of yourself, or of your doings, or of your family, unless there is real necessity for doing so, and then be as brief, as reserved as possible. If others seem to you to talk too much about themselves, try to view their conduct in a favorable light; but do not copy it, even though their words may tend to self-humiliation and self-condemnation.

Rarely speak of your neighbor and of his affairs, unless, indeed, an opportunity offers of saying something in his favor.

Be ready to speak of God, and especially of His Love and Goodness, but with guardedness, lest you fall into some error concerning Him; and rather delight to hear others speak of Him, treasuring up their words in your inmost heart.

Let the sound of men's words strike only upon your ear, and let your heart be lifted up to God; and, if you must listen to what they say in order to know how to reply to them, still forget not to raise your eyes thoughtfully towards Heaven, where God dwells, and contemplate His loftiness, as He deigns to regard your vileness.

Whatever comes into your mind for you to speak, ponder over it well before you utter it, for you will discover that much which you were going to say had better remain unspoken. Indeed I go further, and assure you, that not a few of those things, which you have after consideration spoken, would have been better if they had been consigned to silence; and the truth of this you will perceive, if, when the occasion for speaking is past, you reflect upon what you have said.

Silence, beloved, is a safe stronghold in the spiritual battle, and a sure pledge of victory.

Silence is the friend of him who distrusts self and trusts in God; it is the guardian of the spirit of prayer, and a wonderful help in the attainment of virtues.

If you would learn to bridle your tongue, think often upon the evils and dangers of talkativeness, and the great advantages of silence. Love this virtue; and from time to time (in order to gain the habit of it) keep silence even when you might lawfully speak, provided no prejudice arise from it to your neighbor or to yourself.

And to keep aloof from conversation will be the more helpful, because instead of men, you will have for your companions the Angels, the Saints, and God Himself.

Finally, give yourself to the thought of the conflict in which you are engaged, that, seeing how much lies before you, you may the more easily refrain from overmuch talking.

CHAPTER 25

That the Soldier of Christ, if he would be successful against his
Enemies, must, as far as possible, lay aside All Agitation and Anxiety
of Mind.

SINCE when we have lost peace of mind we should do our best to regain
it, so should we learn that there is absolutely nothing which ought to rob us
of it, or even disturb it.

We have just cause to grieve over our sins, but this sorrow should be
calm, as we have already shown in more than one place. And so our
sorrow for the sins of all others should be a tranquil sorrow—pitying them
with a holy feeling of charity, and lamenting, at least inwardly, over their
offences.

As to other sad and distressing events, as illness, bodily injuries, death of
nearest relatives, pestilences, wars, fires, or such like misfortunes, which are
painful to nature and shunned by the men of the world, we are fully able by
Divine Grace not only to accept, but also to embrace them, as just
punishments to the wicked and opportunities of virtue to the good.

It is in this light our Lord God Himself views them with approbation;
and if we would only follow His Will, then we should pass through all the
troubles and vexations of this life with a calm and peaceful spirit.

And know, as a certainty, that all anxiety of mind is displeasing in His
Divine Sight, whatever may be the cause of it, for it is never free from
imperfection, and always springs from some evil root of self-love.

Keep therefore a sentinel always on the watch, who shall give the alarm
as soon as he discovers any cause of trouble or agitation, that you may take
up arms in self-defense.

And remember, that all these evils, and others like them, are not really
evils, though outwardly they may seem so, neither can they deprive us of
any real good, but are ordered or permitted by God for the just ends which
I have mentioned, or for other purposes which are not revealed to us, but
which are doubtless most just and holy.

Thus may the most unfortunate occurrence become productive of much
good to us, if we will only keep our mind calm and restful; otherwise all our
efforts will be of little or no use.

For when the heart is thus agitated, it is always exposed to various
assaults of the Enemy; and in such a state we cannot discern the right path
and the sure road to holiness. Our Enemy, who hates this peace above all
things, knowing it to be a mark of the indwelling of the Holy Spirit, Who
works in it great wonders, often, under the guise of a friend, tries to deprive
us of it, by stirring up sundry desires within us which present themselves
under the appearance of good; but their deceptive nature may be discovered
by this test amongst others, that they rob us of peace of mind.

In order, therefore, to avert so great an evil, when the sentinel gives notice of any fresh desire, do not admit it into your heart, until you have first, free from all self-seeking and self-will, laid it before God; and, confessing your own ignorance and blindness about it, have earnestly besought Him to show you, whether the desire comes from Him, or from your adversary. And, if possible, obtain also the judgment of your spiritual father in this matter.

Moreover, even if the desire does come from God, yet be careful, before you follow it, to restrain all impetuosity; because the work which is entered upon in a mortified spirit, will be far more acceptable to Him, than that which is undertaken with natural eagerness. And often the mortification is more pleasing in His sight than the work itself.

Thus, rejecting all desires not good, and not acting upon the good ones until you have first curbed your natural impulses, you will be enabled to possess the fortress of your heart in peace and safety.

If you would keep it in perfect peace, you must take care also to guard and defend it from certain stings of conscience and feelings of remorse, which are sometimes from the Devil, although, as they accuse us of some moral failure, they seem to come from God. By their fruits you shall know their source. If they humble you, if they make you diligent in good works, if they do not rob you of your trust in God, then may you thankfully receive them as from God. But if they occasion anxiety, and render you fearful, doubtful, slothful, and backward in well-doing, be assured that they come from the Enemy; do not listen to them, but go on with what you are doing.

Moreover, disquietude arises still more commonly from the approach of adverse events. In order to defend ourselves against this form of attack, there are two things for us to do: one is to consider and find out what is chiefly hindered by these events, our spiritual life, or our self-love and self-will. For if they wound our self-will and self-love (our first and greatest foe) they must not be called adverse, but be regarded as special favors and aids from the Most High God, and therefore be received with a joyful and a thankful heart.

And if they are adverse to the spiritual life, you must not even then suffer your peace of mind to be destroyed, as I will show in the following chapter.

The second thing is to lift up your heart to God, and, with your eyes closed, to accept all things from the compassionate Hand of His Divine Providence, as from a Hand full of manifold blessings, of which, though as yet you do not understand them, you are content to know nothing further.

CHAPTER 26

What we must do when we are Wounded.

WHEN you feel yourself wounded, from having through your weakness, or even through willfulness it may be, fallen into some sin, do not be discouraged nor be over-anxious, but turn at once to God, and say unto Him: "Behold, O Lord, what of myself I have done; what else could be expected of me but falls?"

Then, pausing a little, humble yourself in your own eyes, bewail the offence which you have committed against your Lord, and without discouragement rouse your indignation against your vicious passions, and especially against that one which caused your fall.

Then say: "And not even here, Lord, should I have stopped, if Thou of Thy goodness had not held me back!"

After this, render Him greater thanks and love than ever, wondering at the greatness of His clemency in extending to you His right Hand to save you from another fall, when you had just offended Him.

Lastly, say, with full confidence in His Infinite Mercy: "Forgive me, O Lord, according to Thy Mercy; let me never depart from Thee nor be separated from Thee, and suffer me never to offend Thee any more."

When this has been done, do not sit down to consider whether God has pardoned you or not; for this is only pride, anxiety, restlessness, waste of time, and, under color of various pretexts, a snare of the Devil. But commit yourself freely into the merciful Hands of God, and pursue your course, as if you had not fallen.

And if you should fall many times and receive many wounds in one day, do what I have told you, with the same confidence, the second, third, or even last time, as at the first; despising yourself, and detesting your sin, strive to live more watchfully.

This way of taking falls is very displeasing to the Devil, both because he sees it to be very pleasing to God, and because he is thereby baffled and conquered by the one whom at first he succeeded in conquering. And, therefore, he adopts many artful devices for the purpose of leading us to relinquish it, and is often successful through our carelessness and too little watchfulness over ourselves. The more difficult you find this exercise, the more severely must you deal with yourself, renewing it again and again, even after a single fall.

If, after a fall, you feel anxious, disturbed, and fearful, the first thing to aim at is the recovery of peace and tranquility of mind, and with it, your trustfulness. Furnished with these arms, turn again to the Lord; for your distress about your sin was occasioned, not by the consideration of the offence against God, but of the loss to yourself.

To recover this peace, you must for the time wholly forget your fall, and fix your mind on the unspeakable Goodness of God; considering His great readiness and eagerness to pardon every sin, however grievous; and how He calls the sinner by various means and many ways to return to Him, that He may unite him to Himself in this life, and by grace sanctify him, and in the life to come by His Glory may make him blessed for ever.

When you have quieted your mind with these and similar reflections, think once more upon your fault, doing as I have already bidden you.

Again, at the times of sacramental confession (and I recommend you often to resort to this) look again at your falls, and with renewed sorrow and displeasure for having offended God, and with a resolve never to offend Him more, open them with all simplicity before your spiritual father.

CHAPTER 27

Of the Order which the Devil observes in his Assaults and Stratagems against those who give themselves to a Holy Life, and those who are already found in the Bondage of Sin.

YOU must know, beloved, that the Devil seeks nothing but our ruin, and that he does not use the same plan of assault with all.

In order to describe to you some of his modes of attack, His devices and wiles, I will set before you several conditions of men.

Some are yet in the bondage of sin, and without a thought of leaving it.

Others desire to be free, but never make an attempt to get so.

Others, again, imagine that they are walking in the way of holiness, while they are wandering away far from it.

Others, lastly, after having attained a high degree of virtue, fall into greater ruin.

We will speak of each separately.

CHAPTER 28

Of the Assaults and Devices which the Devil employs against those who are held in the Bondage of Sin.

WHEN the Devil holds any one in the bondage of sin, his great concern is to turn away his mind from every thought which might lead him to discover his most unhappy condition.

And not only does he divert the mind from all thoughts and godly inspirations which may call him to repentance, by instilling thoughts foreign to the subject; but by occasions, ready and prepared for him, he makes him fall into his old sins, or even into worse ones.

Thus, his blindness waxing thicker and denser, he more deeply plunges into a headlong and reckless course of sin, and passing from one stage of darkness to another, and from sin to fouler sin, his wretched life like a wheel runs on even to death, unless God of His grace should provide some means of stopping him.

The remedy for one in this unhappy state, on his side, is to be ready to listen to every whisper and godly inspiration which calls him from darkness to light, crying with all his heart to his Creator, "O my Lord, help me, help me speedily; leave me not any longer in this darkness of sin." Let him never grow weary of repeating this prayer, and of others like it, but cry over and over again.

And, if possible, let him have recourse without a moment's delay to some spiritual father, and ask for counsel and assistance, that he may be delivered from the Enemy.

But if this cannot be done at once, let him promptly cast himself before the Crucified, and there prostrating himself at His Sacred Feet, let him cry for mercy, and ask also for the pity and aid of the Mother of God.

And be assured that in doing this immediately, lies the victory, as you will learn from the next chapter.

CHAPTER 29

Of the Wiles and Delusions by which the Devil holds captive those
who are conscious of their Misery, and desire to be free; and how it is
our Resolutions are so often fruitless.

THOSE who know their evil life, and desire to change it, are often ensnared and overcome by the Devil by such weapons as these:

"Not now, not now."

"Cras, cras," is the raven's cry ("tomorrow, tomorrow"). "I must first settle this or that, arrange my affairs, remove this obstacle, and then I shall be able to attend to spiritual matters with greater tranquility."

This is a snare which has caught, and still catches a vast number of people; and its success arises from our own negligence and carelessness, which make us, in a business in which both the honor of God and the salvation of our soul are at stake, so slow to seize that most powerful weapon "Now, now," wherefore "not now?"

"Today, today," wherefore "tomorrow?" saying to yourself, "Even supposing this 'by and by,' this 'tomorrow,' be granted me, is it a safe course, and the way of victory, to choose first to be wounded and to be guilty of fresh irregularities?"

You see, then, beloved, that to escape this snare, and to overcome the enemy, the remedy is, as has been already mentioned, instant correspondence with the Divine suggestions and inspirations; ready obedience to them, I say, and not mere resolves, for these often are deceptive, and many from various causes have remained deceived by them.

The first reason is, as above referred to, that our good resolves are not based upon self-distrust and trust in God. Our excessive pride—which is the source of this delusion and blindness—hinders us from discovering this. The light which discloses the evil and the medicine which cures it, both come from the goodness of God, Who suffers us to fall that He may lead us from trust in self to trust in Him Alone, and from pride to self-knowledge.

Your resolutions, therefore, to be effectual, must be firmly made; and this they cannot be, unless they are freed from all trust in self, and are humbly based upon trust in God.

The second reason is, that when we make our resolutions, we dwell on the beauty and value of virtue, and these draw out our will, frail and slack as it is; but when we come to face the difficulties which must be surmounted before the virtue can be attained, our will, being weak and inexperienced, fails, and shrinks back from the effort.

Accustom yourself, therefore, to love the difficulties which accompany the attainment of virtues, even more than the virtues themselves; and use these difficulties, now a little and now much, so as to strengthen your will, if you really desire to acquire these virtues. Know also, that the more generously you embrace and value these difficulties, the more speedy and complete shall be your victory over yourself and your enemies.

The third reason is, that in making our resolutions we are prone to keep in view not the virtue and the Divine Will, but our own interest. This is often the case with resolutions which we form in times of spiritual joy or crushing trial, when we feel nothing bring us relief, but the resolve to give ourselves wholly to God, and to the practice of virtue.

In order to avoid this danger, be in times of spiritual delight very cautious and humble in your resolutions, and especially as to promises and vows. And in trial, let your resolutions be to bear your cross patiently, according to the Will of God, and to exalt it, refusing all earthly and sometimes even heavenly consolation. Let your one desire and your one prayer be, that God would enable you to bear all adversity without marring the virtue of patience, and without any thing that may displease your Lord.

CHAPTER 30

Of the Delusion of those who imagine that they are going on to
Perfection.

OUR Enemy, when he is repulsed in his first and second assault and stratagem, has in his malice recourse to a third, which is, to keep our eyes fixed on some higher degree of perfection, making us aspire to and aim after it, and thus rendering us forgetful of the enemies who are close at hand and are actually assaulting and injuring us.

Hence we are continually wounded, but pay no regard to our wounds; and, estimating our intentions as if they were fulfilled, we are filled with various feelings of pride.

Thus, while we will not brook the least contradiction of word or deed, we spend our time in making long meditations and resolutions about bearing sufferings sharper than those which shall be hereafter, for the love of God. And because our lower nature, in the case of pains which are so far off, feels no repugnance to them, therefore do we poor creatures flatter ourselves, that we are already to be classed with those who endure agonies patiently.

To avoid this snare, resolve to fight against those enemies who are close at hand, and are really attacking you. You will in this way discover whether your resolutions are true or deceptive, strong or frail; and you will travel on towards virtue and perfection, by the well-beaten and royal road.

But with regard to enemies who are not now wont to harass you, unless you foresee that they are likely at some time hence to do so, I do not advise you to offer battle; you may, however, make resolutions beforehand, that you may then be found prepared and strong.

Let not your resolutions be estimated by their effects, even though you should have long and rightly exercised yourself in virtue, but be humble as to them, and distrust yourself and your own weakness; and, putting your trust in God, with frequent prayers, fly to Him for succor and protection from dangers, and especially from the danger of the very least presumption and self-confidence.

But in the case of slight defects, which sometimes the Lord permits to remain unconquered in order to increase our self-knowledge or to guard some other good in us, it is notwithstanding allowable to form resolutions of attaining to some higher degree of perfection.

CHAPTER 31

*Of the Devil's Deceits and Struggles to draw us away from the Path
of Perfection.*

THE fourth deceit of the Evil One, as I have already mentioned, is to excite within us, when he sees us steadily advancing in holiness, sundry good desires, in order to lead us from the practice of virtues into wickedness.

A sick person, for instance, is bearing his illness all the while with a patient will. Our cunning adversary, knowing that the sick man may thus attain to the habit of patience, suggests at once to him how much good he might have done under different circumstances, and persuades him that in health he would have served God, and have benefited himself and others, to a greater extent. Having excited these thoughts within him, he goes on increasing them by degrees, till at last he makes him restless at not being able to carry these desires into good effect.

The keener and stronger such desires become the more this restlessness increases. Then, imperceptibly and artfully, the Enemy leads him on to impatience under his sickness, not on account of the sickness itself, but because of the hindrance the sickness becomes to those good works which the sick man so anxiously desires to perform for some greater good.

Having led him on thus far, with the same subtlety he withdraws from his mind the end he had in view, of serving God and doing good works, leaving only the bare desire to be cured of his sickness; and then, when this desire is not granted him, he is vexed, and becomes actually impatient about it. Thus, insensibly he falls from the virtue of which he was acquiring the habit, into the opposite vice.

This is the way to guard against and resist this snare. Be very careful not to allow, when in this state of trial, any desires or projects which you cannot at once carry into effect, and which on that account are likely to disturb you.

In this case resign yourself with all patience, humility, and resignation to the conviction that your desires may after all not have the effect which you supposed, inasmuch as you are weaker and more unstable than you thought yourself to be.

Or else think that perhaps God, in His secret counsels, or for your unworthiness, does not intend you to do this good work, but rather intends you to patiently humble and abase yourself under the loving and mighty hand of His Will.

In like manner, when your spiritual father hinders you, or some other cause, from such frequent attendance at your devotions, and especially the Holy Communion, as you would wish, do not allow yourself to be vexed and disturbed on that account, but give up entirely your own mind, and be clothed with the good pleasure of your Lord, and say—"If the eye of

Divine Providence did not discover in me some ingratitude or defect, I should not now be debarred from receiving this most Holy Sacrament. I see that my Lord thus makes known to me my unworthiness, and therefore I will praise and bless His Name for ever. I am fully persuaded, O my Lord, that in Thy infinite Goodness Thou wilt grant me a heart open and ready to do all Thy good pleasure with resignation and obedience, and that Thou, coming to me spiritually, wilt comfort and strengthen it against all the enemies who would fain separate it from Thee. Thus may it be, as it seems good in Thy Sight. O my Creator and Redeemer, may Thy Will be now and evermore my food and support! This only do I ask of Thee, O my Beloved, that my soul, cleansed and purified from every thing that is displeasing in Thy Sight, and adorned with holy virtues, may be ever prepared for Thy coming, and for the performance of Thy Will, whatsoever it may be."

If you will bear in mind these warnings, know assuredly, that when baffled in any good which you had proposed to do—whether the hindrance be from your own nature, or from the Evil Spirit's endeavor to distress you and turn you aside from the path of holiness, or from God Himself for a trial of your submission to His Will—you will always find an opportunity of pleasing your Lord in some way most acceptable to Him. And in this lies that true devotion and service which God requires of us.

I caution you, further, lest you grow impatient under trials, from whatsoever source they spring, that, in using the lawful means which God's servants are wont to resort to, you do not employ simply with the hope and desire of gaining relief, but because it is the Will of God that you should use them; for we know not whether it will please His Divine Majesty by this means to free us from our troubles. From any other way of acting you will fall into further evils; for if the thing did not turn out according to your mind and desire, you would easily grow impatient, or your patience would have some defect about it, and not be wholly pleasing to God, and would be of little worth.

Lastly, I would warn you against a hidden deceit of our self-love, which is wont under certain circumstances to excuse and justify our faults. Thus, for example, a sick man, who is very impatient under his affliction, conceals his impatience under the cloak of zeal for some apparent good. He says that his vexation does not arise from real impatience at the pain he has to suffer in consequence of the disease, but is a reasonable grief, because he has brought it upon himself, or else because others who wait on him are being worn out and injured.

Thus the ambitious man, who frets that he has failed to gain some honor, does not attribute his discontent to his own wounded pride, but to certain other causes, which he knows very well, at another time when they did not bring trouble upon himself, would give him no concern; so neither would the sick man care, if those about whom he has expressed so much sorrow for their fatigue on his behalf, had incurred the same amount of labor and hurt in waiting upon some one else. This is a clear proof that the root of such men's sorrow is not their concern for others, or for any thing else, but their dislike to have their own will thwarted.

Therefore, in order to escape this and other errors, bear with patience every trouble and sorrow, as I have told you, from whatever cause it may spring.

CHAPTER 32

Of the last above-named Assault and Stratagem, whereby the Devil tries to make the Virtues we have acquired the Occasions of our Ruin.

THE crafty and malicious serpent fails not to tempt us by his subtle devices through the virtues we have acquired. With these he would work our ruin, by inducing us to think too much of them or of ourselves, and thus would lead us to lift up ourselves on high, and thereby to fall into the sin of pride and vainglory.

To protect yourself from this danger, always fight your own battle, placing yourself on the safe and level ground of a true and deep conviction that you are nothing, that you know nothing, that you can do nothing, and that you have nothing of your own but misery and imperfection, and that you deserve nothing but eternal damnation.

Secure and entrench yourself within the bounds of this truth, and never suffer yourself to be drawn aside one single hair's-breadth from it, by any thought or any events which may happen to you, being convinced that such are only so many enemies who want to slay and wound you, if they could only get you into their hands.

If you would exercise yourself well in this field of the knowledge of your own nothingness, use the following rule:

Whenever you are occupied with the thought of yourself or of your own doings, ever reflect upon what you are of yourself, and not upon what is of God and of His grace; and then estimate yourself, according to that only which you are of yourself.

If you consider the time before you were created, you will see that through all that abyss of eternity you were absolutely nothing, and that you did nothing, and could in no way minister to your own creation.

And now, through the Goodness of God only, having been created, if you leave to Him that which is His—His continual Government, whereby He sustains you every moment—what are you of yourself now but still equally nothing?

For it is certain, that, if He were for the slightest moment to withdraw from you, you would return to your original nothingness, out of which His

Almighty Hand drew you. It is clear, then, that you have no ground in this natural being, viewed by itself alone, either for thinking highly of yourself, or for wishing others to think highly of you.

As to that blessed gift of grace within you, or the good works you have been enabled to perform, what good or meritorious action could you by your natural strength have ever done, if you had been deprived of Divine assistance?

If, on the other hand, you call to mind the number of your past faults, and the multitude of sins of which, but for the merciful Hand of God holding you back, you would also have been guilty, you will find, by reckoning up the days and years as well as the acts and habits of sin (for one vice draws another after it) that your iniquities will have become, as it were, innumerable, so that you would be changed into another infernal Lucifer. If, therefore, you would not rob God of His Glory, but ever cleave to your Lord, you must learn day by day to think worse of yourself.

Be careful to deal honestly in the judgment you pass upon yourself, or else you may incur no little harm. For although by this knowledge of your own wickedness you may surpass another, who in his blindness imagines himself to be something, yet you will lose much, and make yourself worse than he is in the motives of your heart, if you desire to be esteemed by men, and to pass for that which you know you are not.

If, then, you wish that this knowledge of your sinfulness and vileness may protect you from your enemies, and make you dear to God, you must not only strive to despise yourself, as unworthy of all good, and deserving of all evil, but you must love to be despised by others, detesting their compliments, delighting in their blame, and stooping, whenever an opportunity offers, to do that which others regard with contempt.

And, lest you should be deterred from this wholesome exercise, pay no account to the judgment which others may form of you, but go on with what you are doing, with the simple view of your own self-abasement and discipline; beware, however, of that presumptuous spirit and subtle pride, which oftentimes, under some specious pretext, causes us to disregard the opinions of others.

Keep firm and recollected within yourself, if at any time it should happen to you to be loved, or regarded as good by others, for some grace which God has bestowed upon you, and do not allow yourself to be drawn aside one step from that which is true and right as to your own nothingness, but turn first to God, and say to Him from your heart, "Keep me, O Lord, from ever robbing Thee of Thy Glory and Grace. To Thee be praise, honor, and glory, but to me confusion of face." Then, turning to him who is praising you, say inwardly, as if addressing him—"How is it that he regards me as good, when in reality my God Alone and His works are good?"

Humble yourself in this manner, and give to the Lord that which is His own, and thus you will put to flight your enemies, and fit yourself to receive greater gifts and favors from God.

And if you are tempted to vanity by looking back upon some good works you have done, regard them at once as God's works, and not your own, and say in your heart, as if addressing them—"I know not how ye did appear or begin to be in my mind, for ye did not derive your origin from me; but the good God and His Grace created, nourished and preserved you. Him only, then, will I acknowledge as your true and first Father, Him will I thank, and to Him will I give all praise on your account."

Consider, then, that not only do all the works which you have done fall short of the light and grace which has been bestowed upon you, in order that you may have the knowledge and power to do them, but that they are exceedingly imperfect, and greatly lack that pure intention, proper care and fervency, accompanied with which they should be wrought.

If you will look at them in this light, you will find cause for shame rather than complacency, for it is but too true that the graces which were pure and perfect when they came from God are sullied by out imperfect use of them.

After this, compare your works with those of the Saints, and other servants of God; for by such a comparison you will clearly see that your best and greatest deeds are of much baser metal, and of little worth.

Then, proceed to compare them with those which Christ wrought for you in the Mysteries of His Life and of His continuous Cross; consider His works in themselves apart from His Divinity, and in the affection and purity of that love with which He wrought them, and you will clearly see that all your works are precisely nothing.

And lastly, if you will lift up your thoughts to the Divinity and boundless Majesty of your God, and to the service which He deserves, you will plainly perceive, that the amount of what you have done for Him ought rather to be a ground of considerable fear than of vanity. Therefore, in all your ways, in all your works, however holy they may be, you must cry unto the Lord with all your heart: "God, be merciful to me, a sinner."

I would further counsel you to be reserved in speaking of the gifts which God has given you, for to publish them is almost always displeasing to your Lord, as He Himself clearly teaches us in the following lesson.

Appearing, as it is said, once to a devout and pure creature of His in the form of a little child, she asked him, with much simplicity, to repeat the Angelical Salutation. He at once began: "Hail, Mary, full of grace, the Lord is with thee, blessed art thou among women"; then He stopped, unwilling to praise Himself in the words which follow. And whilst she was urging Him to proceed, He withdrew from her, leaving His servant full of consolation, because of the heavenly doctrine which, by His example, He had taught her.

Do you also, beloved, learn to humble yourself, and to acknowledge yourself to be nothing, and your works to be nothing also. This is the foundation of all other virtues.

God, when we had no being, created us out of nothing; and now that through Him we have a being, He wills that the whole spiritual fabric should be based on this foundation, namely, the knowledge of our own nothingness. And the deeper this knowledge becomes, the higher will the building rise. And according as we dig out the earth of our own wretchedness, so much the more will the Divine Architect bring the most solid stones to advance the building.

Never imagine, beloved, that you can ever dig deep enough; but, on the contrary, believe this of yourself, that if any thing in a creature could be infinite, it would be your vileness.

With this knowledge, practically carried out, we possess all good; without it, we should be little better than nothing, though we had done all the works of the Saints, and were ourselves continually occupied with God.

O blessed knowledge, which makes us happy on earth and glorious in Heaven! O light, which rises out of darkness, and brightly illuminates the soul! O unspeakable joy, which shines amidst our impurities! O nothingness, which, when known, puts all things in our power!

I should never tire of telling you this: if you will praise God, accuse yourself, and desire to be accused by others. Humble yourself with all, and bend beneath all, if you would exalt Him in yourself and yourself in Him. If you would find Him, exalt not yourself, for if you do, He will fly from you.

Abase yourself, abase yourself to the utmost, and He will seek you and embrace you; and the more you humble yourself in your own sight, and are content to be regarded as worthless by others, and to be cast aside as an abominable thing, the more tenderly and lovingly will He welcome you and draw you to His Side.

Reckon yourself unworthy of this so great a gift which God vouchsafes to you, Who, to unite you to Himself, suffered shame for your sake. Fail not to render to Him continual thanks, and consider yourself under an obligation to those who have given you an opportunity of humbling yourself, and still more to those who have trampled upon you, and who, in addition to this, think that you are not taking it well, but badly. And, even if it is so, you ought to hide the feeling.

If, notwithstanding all these considerations, which are but too true, the subtlety of the Devil, and our own ignorance and bad inclinations, should so prevail within us, that thoughts of our own superiority still disquiet us, and will make their impressions on our hearts, then from that very fact we may draw an argument for humbling ourselves in our own eyes; for such thoughts show us that we are far behind in the spiritual life, and in the true knowledge of ourselves, seeing that we are unable to shake off these annoyances which spring from our empty pride. By this means, from the poison we may extract honey, from the wounds the cure.

CHAPTER 33

Of certain Suggestions for overcoming our Evil Passions, and gaining new Virtues.

ALTHOUGH I have already said so much of the means whereby we may overcome self, and adorn ourselves with virtues, I will yet give you some further cautions.

First, in your endeavors after holiness, never be persuaded to adopt that routine of spiritual exercises, which divides the week, so as to set apart one day for one particular virtue, and another day for another; but let the order of your warfare and exercises be, to war against those passions which have been always injuring you, and which still often attack and injure you, and to adorn yourself with the virtues which are opposite to them, as perfectly as possible.

For when you have gained these virtues, you will have no difficulty in acquiring the rest, as occasion offers; and occasions will present themselves, inasmuch as all the virtues are so interlinked one with another, that you cannot possess one perfectly without having all the rest already, as it were, on the threshold of your heart.

Secondly, never set a fixed time for the attainment of virtues, nor say that you will gain them in so many days, weeks, or years; but, as an infant or a newly-enlisted soldier, fight your way, and push forward towards the summit of perfection.

Do not ever stand still, even for an instant; for to stand still in the way of virtue and perfection, is not to recover breath or courage, but to relapse and grow feebler than before.

By standing still, I mean making yourself believe that you have perfectly gained the virtue, and thus that you need pay little attention to the occasions which may call you to new acts of the virtue, or to slight failures in it.

Therefore be vigilant, fervent, and careful, so as not to miss the least opportunity of exercising a virtue. Embrace every occasion which may lead to it, and especially those which excel in difficulty, because acts which are most difficult to be performed are those which most quickly and thoroughly establish the habit; therefore love those who offer you such opportunities.

But flee those only, and that with rapid step, with all haste and diligence, which may lead to temptations of the flesh.

Thirdly, be prudent and discreet concerning those exercises which may prove injurious to your bodily health, such as self-chastisement with disciplines, haircloth, fastings, vigils, meditations, and the like; for these practices must be discreetly and slowly acquired, as we shall presently show.

Then as to virtues which are wholly internal, such as love of God, contempt of the world, self-abasement, hatred of evil passions and sin, patience and meekness, love for all men, even for those who injure us, and such like; it is not necessary to attain to these by degrees, nor to mount with gradual rise to perfection in them, but strive at once to make each act as perfect as possible.

Fourthly, let your whole mind, desire, and heart be set upon, wish for, and long for nothing but to gain the victory over the passion against which you are struggling, and to form the opposite virtue. Be this your world, your heaven, your earth, your whole treasure; and all with the view of pleasing God. Whether you are eating or fasting, laboring or resting, watching or sleeping, at home or abroad, whether engaged in devotion or in manual labor, let your aim be to overcome and subdue this passion, and to gain the opposite virtue.

Fifthly, be the foe of all earthly pleasures and gratifications, and in this way you will weaken the power of all vices, which have their root in the love of pleasure. Therefore, when this is cut away by hatred of self, they lose their vigor and force.

For if whilst you on the one hand fight against a particular indulgence, and on the other attach yourself to some earthly delight (though it amount only to a venial fault), hard will be the battle, and bloody, and the victory rare and very uncertain.

Therefore bear in mind those divine utterances: "He that loves his life shall lose it, and he that hates his life in this world shall keep it unto life eternal." *St. John* xii. 25. "Brethren, we are debtors not to the flesh, to live after the flesh. For if ye live after the flesh ye shall die; but if ye through the spirit do mortify the deeds of the body, ye shall live." *Rom.* viii. 12.

Sixthly, my last advice is, that you should make a general confession, for this, perhaps, you will find necessary at first, observing all that is required for doing it well; so shall you be more certain that you are in your Lord's favor, from Whom alone all graces and all victories must be looked for.

CHAPTER 34

*That Virtues are to be gained by degrees; by Exercising ourselves in
their gradual formation, and that our Attention must first be given to
one step, and then to another.*

ALTHOUGH the true soldier of Christ, who aspires to the height of
perfection, should not assign limits to his progress, still there are some
forms of spiritual fervor which need to be checked with a certain discretion,
lest, being ardently embraced at first, they should be soon exhausted, and
thus desert us in the middle of our course. Therefore, besides what has
been said about moderation in external exercises, we must also learn, that
even interior virtues had better be acquired by degrees, and step by step; for
in this way that which is small soon becomes great and abiding. Thus, for
example, we should not as a rule practice patience in the high degree, which
consists in rejoicing in afflictions and desiring them, before we have passed
through the lower degrees of the virtue.

Neither do I advise you to endeavor to give your attention to all the
virtues at once, but to one only, and afterwards to others; for thus the habit
of virtue is more easily and firmly rooted in the soul. If you are striving to
acquire one particular virtue, you remember it more readily on all occasions;
your mind too is sharpened by the discovery of new ways and motives for
cultivating it, and the will bends itself more easily and earnestly in the
pursuit of it, than if it were occupied with many virtues at once.

And with this uniform exercise, the acts which concern one single virtue
are performed with less fatigue, in consequence of their resemblance to one
another. The performance of one act facilitates the performance of the
next, which is like unto it; and by this common likeness they make a deeper
impression on us, the seat of the heart being already prepared and disposed
for receiving those which are newly produced, having already made room
for similar acts before.

These reasons have the greater force, as it is quite certain that every one
who practices himself in one virtue at the same time learns the exercise of
the rest; and thus, through the inseparable bond which exists between them,
when one virtue grows the rest increase with it, as rays proceeding from one
and the same Divine Light.

CHAPTER 35

*Of the Means by which Virtues are acquired, and of the Way we
should Use them, allowing some space of Time to one Virtue only.*

FOR the pursuit of virtues, besides all that has been said above, we need a
large and generous mind; a will, neither unstable nor remiss, but resolute
and strong, with the certain persuasion that many hindrances and trials have
to be overcome.

There are, moreover, particular inclinations and affections which we
may gain, by frequently considering how pleasing they are to God, how
noble and excellent in themselves, and how profitable and necessary for us,
for from them all perfection has its origin and end.

Each morning, then, make a steadfast resolve to exercise yourself in
them during the day, according to the events which are likely to happen
during the day; and often, as it passes, examine yourself in order to see
whether you have kept your resolution or not; and renew it with fresh
earnestness. And this should be done especially with regard to the
particular virtue which we are endeavoring to acquire.

Let the examples of the Saints, and our meditations and prayers on the
Life and Passion of Christ (so needful in every spiritual exercise), be all
applied principally to the virtue which we have made it our task to practice.

Let the same be done on all occasions (as we shall presently explain
more particularly), however different they may be from one another.

Let us take pains to accustom ourselves to interior and exterior acts of
virtue, that we may be enabled to perform them with the same facility and
readiness, as we did those which accorded with our natural will. And (as we
have said elsewhere) the more these acts are contrary to the natural will, the
more quickly will they produce the good habit in the soul.

The sacred words of the Divine Scriptures, uttered by the voice, or at
least with the mind, and selected according to the occasion, have a
wonderful power to aid us in this exercise.

We ought therefore to keep such texts in readiness as bear upon the
virtue we are practicing, and let them be repeated during the day, especially
whenever the opposite passion begins to assert itself.

Thus, for example, if we are trying to gain patience, we can use the
following words, or others like them:

"My children, suffer patiently the wrath that is come upon you from
God." *Baruch* x. 25.

"The expectation of the poor shall not perish for ever." *Psalm* ix. 18.

"He that is slow to anger is better than the mighty; and he that rules his
spirit than he that takes a city." *Proverbs* xvi. 32.

"In your patience possess ye your souls." *St. Luke* xxi. 19.

"Let us run with patience the race that is set before us." *Hebrews* xii. 1.

For the same purpose we may say the following, or some similar short prayers:

"When, O my God, shall this heart of mine be armed with the shield of patience?"

"When, to content my Lord, shall I be able to endure every trial with an undisturbed mind?"

"Oh! sufferings most precious, which make me like my Lord Jesus, enduring the Passion for me!"

"Oh! Only Life of my soul, will it ever come to pass that I could live in contentment amidst a thousand torments for Thy Glory!"

"Happy should I be, if in the midst of the furnace of affliction, I could still burn with the desire of enduring greater things!"

We should use these short prayers, or others like them, which help towards the attainment of virtues, and are calculated to cherish the spirit of devotion.

These short prayers are called ejaculations, because they are shot like darts or arrows towards Heaven.

They have a great effect upon us, stirring us to virtue, and penetrate even to the heart of God, if they have, so to speak, these two wings: one, a true knowledge that God is pleased with such spiritual exercises; the other, a true and ardent desire after holiness with the sole end of pleasing His Divine Majesty.

CHAPTER 36

That in the Exercise of Virtue we must continually Advance with Diligence.

AMONGST the things which are most important and necessary for the attainment of virtues, besides those already taught, this is to be borne in mind—that we must uninterruptedly press forward towards the end we have purposed; else, by only standing still, we turn back.

For as soon as we leave off acts of virtue, it follows of necessity, that, by the violent inclination of the sensual appetite and the action of external objects, many unruly passions are raised in us, which impair or destroy holiness; and, besides that, we lose many graces and gifts, which, if we had continued to press onward, we might have gained from the Lord. In this respect the spiritual traveler is unlike the one who performs an earthly journey, for the latter may rest without losing the ground he has gained, while with the former this would be impossible. There is another difference too between them: the weariness of the earthly traveler increases with the continuance of the bodily exertion, while in the spiritual journey, the longer the traveler walks the more strength and vigor he gains. For by the habit of virtue, the lower nature, which by its rebellion at first makes the way rough and toilsome, is gradually weakened; while the higher nature, in which virtue resides, gets more firm and more robust.

Therefore, as we progress in holiness, the pain which we felt lessens, and a certain secret joy, which, by the Divine working had intermingled with it, increases more and more.

In this way, by steadily going on from one virtue to another, we arrive at last at the summit of the mountain, where the perfected soul can work without weariness, nay, with pleasure and joyfulness; because, having now conquered and tamed its unruly passions, and having risen above all created things and above itself, it lives happily in the Heart of the Most High, and there, sweetly laboring, finds its repose.

CHAPTER 37

That as we must always continue in the Exercise of the Virtues, so we must not shun any Opportunity which offers itself for their Attainment.

WE have clearly seen, that in the path of holiness we must ever press onward without stopping. Therefore we ought to be watchful and expectant, lest we let slip any opportunity which may present itself for the increase of a virtue; and those who draw back from such contrary things as might serve to that purpose, make a great mistake.

For if you desire (not to depart from the virtue which has provided us with an example hitherto) to grow in the habit of patience, it is not well to keep away from the persons, deeds, or thoughts, which try your patience.

Therefore you have no need to give up any of your associations, because they are tiresome to you; but whilst you are dealing with and concerned with whatever brings you annoyance, keep your will disposed and ready to endure whatever vexation or unpleasantness may come to you; else you will never get the habit of patience.

If any employment be irksome to you, either on its own account, or because of the person who laid it on you; or, if you dislike it, because it hinders you from doing what you like better, still undertake it and complete it, whatever trouble it be to you, and though you might find comfort by not doing it. Because if you leave it, you would never learn to suffer, neither would true peace ever be your portion, as it does not spring except from a soul purified from passion and adorned with holiness.

The same holds good of harassing thoughts, which at times molest and disturb the mind. You need not drive them entirely away, for, together with the pain they cause you, they accustom you to bear contradictions.

Whoever gives you different advice, teaches you rather to shun the pain you feel, than to gain the virtue which you desire.

True, indeed, it is that a young soldier ought to maneuver and guard himself with watchfulness and dexterity on such occasions, now facing the enemy, now retiring, as he gains more or less spiritual strength and power; yet he must never quite turn away and retreat, so as to place himself far from all opportunity of contradiction: for though for the time he might save himself from falling, in the future he would run a greater risk, when exposed to the assaults of impatience, from not having armed and strengthened himself beforehand with the practice of the contrary virtue.

This advice, however, must not be followed when sins of the flesh are concerned, of which we have before spoken more particularly.

CHAPTER 38

That we ought to regard as precious every Opportunity which is afforded to us for the Acquisition of Virtues; and chiefly those which present the greatest Difficulties.

THAT you should accept the opportunities which present themselves of acquiring virtue is not enough, beloved; you should also sometimes seek them, as things of great price and value, and ever embrace them joyfully as soon as they appear; and the more distasteful they are to nature, the more dear and precious should they be esteemed. This, by the Divine assistance, you will be enabled to do, if you will bear in mind the following considerations.

One is, that opportunities are means adapted, nay, necessary for acquiring virtues. Hence, when you are seeking virtues from the Lord, you are by a necessary consequence asking also for opportunities, else your prayer would be vain, and you would be contradicting your own words and tempting God, for He ordinarily does not give patience without tribulation, nor humility without humiliations.

The same may be said of all other virtues, which are doubtless only to be gained by adverse circumstances; and the more painful these are, the more effectually do they aid us, and therefore the more acceptable and welcome should they be.

For acts of virtue, done in such cases, are more heroic and generous, and more easily and quickly open to us the way to holiness.

But even the slightest opportunity, though but a word or look, which crosses our will, should be prized and not allowed to pass unused; for such acts, though less intense than those made in the face of considerable difficulties, are more frequent.

Another consideration (of which I have already spoken) is, that every thing which happens to us comes from God for our good, and in order that we may turn it to account.

And although (as we have elsewhere said) some things spring from our own defects, and those of others, and therefore cannot be said to be of God, Who wills nothing that is sinful, yet are they from God, inasmuch as He permits them, and does not prevent them, though He has it in His power to do so.

But all sorrows and afflictions, whether they are the result of our own fault, or of the malice of others, are both from God, and of God; because He concurs in them, and that which He would not have us do as being utterly hateful and abominable in His most pure eyes, He yet wills that we should suffer, both for our quicker growth in holiness, and for other wise reasons unknown to us.

If, then, it is most certainly our Lord's Will that we should cheerfully endure all crosses which may come to us, either from our own evil doings, or from those of others, for us to say—as many say as an excuse for their impatience—that God wills not, nay, hates evil deeds, is but a vain pretext for hiding our own fault, and for refusing the cross which we well know He intended us to bear.

Indeed, I will go further and say, that, taking all things into consideration, our Lord is more pleased with our endurance of those sufferings which come to us from the misdeeds of others, especially from those who are under an obligation to us, than with our endurance of those trails which arise from other distressing accidents. And this because our proud nature is more humbled in the former than in the latter case; and also because, by cheerfully enduring them, we do most especially please and magnify our God, working together with Him in that which renders His unspeakable Goodness and Almightiness most conspicuous, namely, His way of drawing out of the deadly poison of malice and wickedness the sweet and precious fruit of virtue and goodness.

Know, then, beloved, that when the Lord has discovered in us the desire to yield ourselves up in earnest, and to strive as we ought for so great a prize, He at once prepares for us a cup of the sharpest temptations and hardest trials, that we may drink it when He wills; and we, as we acknowledge His love and our own profit, should receive it cheerfully and blindly, and drink it trustingly and unhesitatingly to the very dregs, for it is a medicine, mixed by an unerring Hand, and composed of ingredients which are as profitable to the soul as they are bitter in themselves.

CHAPTER 39

How to avail ourselves of the various Occasions which present themselves for the Exercise of a single Virtue.

IT has been already seen, that it is better to exercise ourselves in a single virtue at a time than in many at once; and that we should use the opportunities we meet with to this end, however various. Now learn how you may effect this with tolerable facility.

It may happen that in the very same day, and perhaps in the same hour, that we are blamed for some good action, or found fault with for some other cause; we may be harshly denied some favor we have asked for, or some trifling request; we may be accused of something we have not done, or be called upon to endure some bodily pain, or some petty annoyance (such as a dish badly cooked); or we may have to bear some real and heavy trial, such as this miserable life is full of.

In this variety of occurrences, and in any other like events, we may perform various acts of virtue, yet, if we would keep to our rule, we must continue to exercise ourselves in acts which belong to the virtue we have in hand.

For example; if it is patience we are endeavoring to cultivate, when these opportunities present themselves, we must meet them with a willing and light heart.

If it is humility, we must in all our troubles acknowledge that we deserve them.

If it is obedience, we must promptly submit ourselves to the Almighty Hand of God, and for His pleasure (since He has so willed it) to all rational and even senseless creatures that may have occasioned us annoyances.

If it is poverty, we shall be quite ready to be stripped of all the consolations of this world, great and small.

If it is charity, we shall perform acts of love towards our neighbor, through whose instrumentality we may thus progress; and towards our Lord God, as the First and Loving Cause, from Whom our discomforts proceed, or by Whom they are permitted to arise, for our discipline and spiritual improvement.

What has been said of the various accidents which may every day happen is equally true of a trial of long continuance, such as sickness, or other like affliction; we may yet go on making acts of the virtue, in which we are at the time exercising ourselves.

CHAPTER 40

*Of the length of time to be given to the Exercise of each particular
Virtue, and of the marks of Spiritual Advancement.*

IT is not for me to determine the length of time to be bestowed upon
acquiring each virtue. In this we must be guided by the state and needs of
each person, by the progress they are making in the spiritual life, and by the
direction of their guide.

But if we set to work in earnest, in the way we have prescribed, there
can be no doubt but that, in a few weeks, we shall have made considerable
progress.

It is a sign of advancement in the spiritual life, if notwithstanding
dryness of spirit, darkness, anguish of soul, and desolation, we yet firmly
persevere in our exercises of virtue.

Another clear indication of growth, is to be found in the degree of
resistance made by our sensual nature to the performance of acts of virtue;
for the weaker the resistance, the greater the progress. When, therefore, we
no longer feel contradiction and rebellion in our lower and sensual nature,
and especially in sudden and unexpected assaults, we may look upon this as
a sign that the virtue we are seeking has been acquired.

And the greater the alacrity and brightness of spirit with which these
acts are done, the greater advantage may we hope to derive from their
exercise.

Beware, however, not to assume as a certainty that we have formed a
virtue, or gained a lasting victory over a passion, even though for a long
time, and after many battles, we may have ceased to feel its motions within
us. For such a result may be brought about by the artifices and workings of
Satan, and of our own deceitful nature; for through our lurking pride we
take that for virtue which is really vice. Besides, if we consider the standard
of perfection to which God calls us, however great our progress may have
been in the way of holiness, we shall hardly persuade ourselves that we have
even crossed its threshold.

As a young soldier, then, and, as it were, a newborn babe in the conflict,
return continually to your earliest exercises, as though as yet you had done
nothing.

And remember, beloved, that it is much better to seek to advance in
virtues, than to examine too nicely what progress you have made; for the
Lord God, the true and only Searcher of our hearts, gives this knowledge to
some and not to others, according as He sees that it will lead to humility or
to pride; and, like a loving Father, He removes a danger from one, whilst to
another He vouchsafes an opportunity of growing in the virtue.

Therefore, though the soul does not perceive the progress which has been made, yet still continue these exercises, for when the Lord wills our progress shall be revealed to us for our greater good.

CHAPTER 41

That we must not yield to the wish to be rid of the Trials which we are bearing patiently; and how we should rule all our Desires so as to grow in Holiness.

WHEN you find yourself in some painful position, and bearing it patiently, be careful lest the Devil, or the suggestions of self-love, lead you to desire to be free from it; for by this two great evils might happen to you.

One is, that if the wish did not altogether destroy the virtue of patience, it would at least gradually dispose you to impatience.

The other, that your patience would become defective, and would be rewarded by God only according to the length of time it was exercised; whereas, if you had not desired the removal of the suffering, but had submitted unreservedly to the Divine Will, your sufferings would have been accepted by God as equivalent to a service of long endurance, though they had lasted but an hour, or even less.

Make this your universal rule in this and in all things, to keep your desires so far withdrawn from every other object, that they may tend simply and purely to their true and only end—the Will of God. For thus will they be holy and just, and you—whatever may happen in a contrary manner—will remain calm and contented; for, as nothing can take place except it be appointed by the Supreme Will, if you will the same, you will come at all times both to will and to have all that happens and all that you desire.

This cannot be understood of your own sins or of those of others, for these God wills not, but it does apply to every chastisement which arises from these or other causes, though it be so severe and searching as to reach to the bottom of the heart, and to wither the very roots of the natural life; for this is the cross with which God is sometimes pleased to favor His nearest and dearest friends.

And what I say of the endurance which we must exercise on all occasions, must be understood also of those remains of any trouble which the Lord wills us to bear, even after we have used all lawful means to be freed from it.

And even in using these means we should be guided by the Providence and Will of God, Who has ordained them, that we might use them according to His Will, and not to please ourselves. Neither should we desire nor love relief from trials, beyond that limit which His service requires and His Will appoints.

CHAPTER 42

How to resist the Devil when he tries to ensnare us by an indiscreet Zeal.

WHEN the Devil, crafty as he is, observes that we are walking straight forward in the path of holiness with lively and well-regulated desires, and that he cannot draw us aside by open allurements, he transforms himself into an angel of light, and by friendly suggestions, quotations from Scripture, and examples of the Saints, importunately urges us to aspire indiscreetly to the height of perfection, that he may presently cause us to fall headlong from it.

With this in view he excites us to chastise the body with great harshness, with scourges, fasts, hair-cloths, and other similar mortifications, that he may either tempt us to pride, by thinking we are doing great things (as is especially the case with women), or that he may undermine our health, and so unfit us for doing good works, or else that spiritual exercises may become irksome and distasteful to us through pain and over-fatigue; and thus by degrees we grow lukewarm in the way of godliness, and at last rush with greater avidity than before to the delights and pleasures of the world.

With many this has been the case. They, having been led on by a presumptuous spirit, and by the impulses of an indiscreet zeal, have, in their excessive outward austerities, gone beyond the measure of their own strength, and so have perished in their own inventions, and have become the sport of malicious fiends. This would never have happened if they had laid to heart what we have been saying and considering, which is, that painful acts of this sort, however praiseworthy and profitable to those whose bodily strength and lowliness of spirit are equal to them, must yet ever be limited by the requirements of each man's constitution and temperament.

And if you cannot imitate the Saints in their austerities, you may find other features in their character which you can copy, by strong and effectual desires and fervent prayers, aspiring after the most glorious crowns of Christ's true soldiers; by despising, as they did, the whole world, and themselves also; by giving themselves up to silence and solitude; by humility and gentleness towards all men; by patience under wrongs, and kindness to those who treated them ill; by watchfulness against even the smallest fault, for this is more pleasing to God than all bodily austerities. I counsel you, then, to be sparing in the use of such, so as to be able, if needs be, to increase your mortification, rather than to run the risk of having to give them up altogether because of excesses. I give you this advice, being persuaded that you are not likely to fall into the error of some, who, though they pass for spiritual persons in the world, yet are they deluded and led astray by their deceitful nature into over-carefulness about the preservation of their bodily health. So jealous and anxious over it are they, that for the most trifling matter they live in fear and dread of losing it. There is nothing they think about more, or are more ready to speak of, than the management of their bodily health. Hence they are also planning how to procure food suited rather to their taste than to their digestion, which latter has often been impaired by their indulgence in delicacies. And, although this is done under the pretext of being able to serve God better, it is but a vain attempt to unite two deadly foes, the spirit and the flesh—an attempt which results in benefiting neither and in injuring both, for this same over-carefulness impairs the health of the one and the devotion of the other.

A certain degree of liberty in these matters is safer and more profitable as a rule; yet it must be accompanied by the discretion of which I have been speaking, and have regard to the differences of constitution and spiritual state, which cannot be subjected to a uniform rule.

Further than this, I would add, that not only in outward things, but also in the pursuit of inward holiness, we should proceed with moderation, as has been shown above, as to the gradual attainment of virtues.

CHAPTER 43

Of the Power of our Evil Inclinations, and of the Way the Devil tempts us to form rash Judgments of our Neighbor, and how to resist him.

FROM the above-named vice of self-esteem and self-conceit arises another most hurtful, namely, the practice of rashly judging our neighbor, which leads us to disparage, despise, and lower him. As this fault springs from pride and evil inclination, so is it thereby willingly cherished and fomented; and our pride increases as the fault increases, and insensibly flatters and deceives us. For the more we presume to exalt ourselves, so much the more do we in our opinion depreciate others, and imagine that we are free from those imperfections which we make ourselves believe we see in them.

And the crafty Devil, who sees this most evil disposition in us, stands ever on the watch to open our eyes and make us quick-sighted to detect, examine, and exaggerate the deficiencies of others.

The careless do not believe or imagine how busy he is in impressing on our minds the little failings of this or that person, when he cannot bring before us great faults.

Seeing, then, that he is so intent on our destruction, let us be watchful, lest we fell into his snares. And as soon as he sets before you any failing of your neighbor, turn away from the thought at once; and if you still feel tempted to criticize, do not yield to the desire. Remember that the right to judge another is not yours; and that even if it had been entrusted to you, you would be incapable of exercising it with integrity, as you are encompassed by a thousand passions, and but too prone to think evil of another without just cause.

The most effectual remedy against this temptation is, I would remind you, the attentive consideration of your own heart; for you will hourly make fresh discoveries of the amount of work you have to do in yourself, and for yourself, which will leave you neither the leisure nor the inclination to busy yourself about the conduct of others.

Moreover, by the faithful performance of this exercise of self-inspection, you will more and more purge your inward eye of those bad humors which foster this pestilent vice of rash judgment.

Know this, too, that when uncharitably you think you see an evil in your brother, some root of the same evil is in your own heart, which, in proportion as it is ill-disposed, readily sees in another that which is already in itself.

When, therefore, we are inclined to judge others for some fault, let us inwardly be indignant with ourselves as guilty of the same, and say in our heart, "How dare I, wretched being, buried in this very fault myself, and in far more grievous ones, lift up my head to see and judge the faults of others?"

And thus the weapons which, when aimed at others, would have wounded you yourself, being used against yourself, bring healing to your wounds.

But if you cannot disguise the fact that your brother has committed a fault, yet take a compassionate view of it, and believe that he has hidden virtues, to guard which the Lord has permitted him to fall; or, that this failing is allowed to cling to him for a time, that he may become more vile in his own sight; or that, being despised by others, he may learn to humble himself, and thus become more pleasing to God, and so his gain at last may become greater than his loss.

If again the sin be not only unmistakable, but grievous, and obstinately persisted in, turn your thoughts to the secret and awful judgments of God; and see how many, once most wicked, attained at last to an eminent degree of sanctity, whilst, on the other hand, many who seemed to have reached sublime heights of perfection, have fallen headlong into misery.

Therefore ever fear and tremble for yourself more than for any other.

And be assured, that every good and kindly feeling towards your neighbor is the work of the Holy Spirit; and that all disparagement, rash judgment, and bitterness against him, owe their origin to the evil that is in ourselves and to the suggestions of the Devil.

If, then, the failings of another have made an impression on you, rest not, nor sleep, until you have, to the utmost of your power, effaced it from your heart.

CHAPTER 44

Of Prayer.

IF distrust of self, trust in God, and spiritual exercises, are so needful as they have been shown to be in this combat, needful above all is prayer (the fourth weapon, mentioned in the beginning of this book), by means of which we may obtain from our Lord, not only the things already named, but all other good things.

For prayer is the means by which we obtain all the graces which rain down upon us from the Divine Fountain of Goodness and Love.

By prayer, if you use it aright, you will put a sword into the Hand of God, with which He will fight and conquer for you; and to use it aright, you must have formed, or be striving to form, the following habits.

First, you must cultivate an earnest desire to serve His Divine Majesty in all things, and in the way which is most pleasing to Him. In order to kindle this desire, consider diligently how worthy beyond expression God is, to be served and honored, because of His wondrous excellences, His Goodness, Majesty, Wisdom, Beauty, and other infinite Perfections.

Consider, too, how to serve you He labored and suffered for three and thirty years, binding and healing the putrefying sores, poisoned with the venom of sin, not with oil and wine and bandages, but with the precious Stream which flowed from His most Sacred Veins, and with His most pure Flesh, torn with scourges, thorns, and nails.

Think, moreover, of the great advantage of this service; for by it we gain the mastery over self, superiority over Satan, and become the sons of God.

Secondly, you must have a lively faith and trust in God, that He will give you all things which you need for His service, and for your own good.

This holy confidence is a vessel into which Divine Mercy pours the treasures of His grace; and the larger and more capacious it is, the more richly laden will our prayers return into our bosom. For how shall the Unchanging and Almighty God fail to impart to us His gifts, when He Himself has commanded us to ask for them, and has also promised us His Holy Spirit, if we ask for it with faith and perseverance?

Thirdly, you must, when you draw nigh in prayer, seek the accomplishment of the Divine Will, and not of your own, both by the act of prayer itself and by that you desire to obtain; that is, pray, as an act of obedience to the Divine Will, and desire to be heard in so far only as God wills. In short, your attention should be to unite your will to God's, not to bend His to yours.

And the reason for this is, that your own will, being tainted and corrupted by self-love, very often errs, and knows not what it asks; but the Divine Will, always united to ineffable Goodness, can never err. Therefore the Will of God ought to be the rule and ruler of all other wills; and deserves and desires to be followed and obeyed by all.

Ask, therefore, such things as you know are conformable to the Divine Will, and if you stand in doubt whether any thing you desire is so or not, ask to obtain it only on the condition of its accordance with the Will of God.

And if we are sure that the things we ask are agreeable to Him, such as virtues, ask for them rather in order to serve and please Him, than for any other motive or end, however spiritual.

Fourthly, if we desire that our prayers should be answered, we must previously adorn ourselves with actions corresponding to our petitions, and, after we have prayed, labor more earnestly to render ourselves fit to receive the grace and virtue we have sought.

For prayer and self-discipline must always go together, and the one revolves round the other; since he who prays for a virtue and makes no effort to practice it, would be rather a tempter of God than any thing else.

Fifthly, before you pray for any thing, make an act of thanksgiving for previous mercies, in this or some similar form of words:

"O Lord, Who of Thy Goodness hast created and redeemed me, and Who, times without number, and when I knew not, hast rescued me out of the hands of my enemies; help me now, and, forgetting all my past rebellion and ingratitude, deny me not my request."

And if you are asking for a particular virtue, and in the midst of the very act of prayer you are tempted by the contrary vice, forget not to thank God for giving you such an opportunity of practicing the virtue you are praying for, and regard it as a special favor on His part.

Sixthly, as the force and efficacy of prayer in bending God to our desires are due to the Bounty and Goodness of His own Nature, to the merits of the Life and Passion of His Only-begotten Son, and to His gracious promise to hear us, we should always conclude our prayer with one or more of the following sentences:

"Of Thy great Mercy, O Lord, grant me this grace." "May the merits of Thy Son obtain for me that which I ask of Thee." "My God, be mindful of Thy promises, and hear my prayer."

And at other times we may also ask for graces through the prayers of the Blessed Virgin and other Saints, who have great power before God, in that He is pleased to honor them now, who honored His Divine Majesty during their sojourn on earth.

Seventhly, we must persevere in prayer, for humble perseverance triumphs over the Invincible One. If the steadfastness and importunity of the widow in the Gospel inclined to her request the judge laden with all iniquity, how should such perseverance fail to move the heart of God, and incline Him to grant our petitions, Who is the Fountain of all Goodness?

And if the Lord should defer answering your prayer, or even seem to reject it, only pray on still, and keep your confidence in His help firm and unshaken; for He possesses, beyond measure, all that is needed to make graces in others.

Therefore, unless there is some impediment on our part, we shall infallibly obtain what we ask, or something else more expedient for us, or it may be both together.

And the more He seems to repel you, the lower should you humble yourself in your own sight, and reflect upon your own unworthiness; yet, keeping your gaze steadfastly fixed on the Mercy of God, increase more and more your confidence in Him, which if you keep lively and unshaken, the more it is assailed, the more pleasing will you become to your Lord.

Give Him, then, continual thanks, confessing Him to be no less Good, Wise, and Loving, when some of your petitions are denied than when they are all granted. Whatever may happen, let us remain steadfast and joyful, in humble submission to His Divine Providence.

CHAPTER 45

What is Mental Prayer.

MENTAL prayer is the lifting up of our heart to God, accompanied with an actual or virtual request for something we desire.

It is an actual request, when we clothe our thought or desire with unspoken words, mentally forming such sentences as these, or others like them: "O Lord, grant me this grace, for Thy Name's Sake"; or, "O Lord, I believe it is in accordance with Thy Will, and for Thy Glory, that I should ask and receive this grace from Thee; accomplish therefore now Thy Divine Will in me."

And when you feel the assaults of your enemies, say thus: "My God, haste Thou to help me, that I yield not to mine enemies"; or, "My God, my Refuge, Thou Strength of my heart, help me speedily, lest I fall." And continue to pray in this way, until the struggle is over, manfully resisting your enemy all the while.

When the heat of the conflict is past, turn to your Lord, and present before Him the enemy who has been attacking you, and your own frailty in resisting him, and say: "See, O Lord, the creature of Thy bounty, which Thou hast made with Thy Hands, and redeemed with Thy Blood. Behold also Thine enemy, who strives to pluck it out of Thine Hand, and to devour it. To Thee, O Lord, I fly for succor, in Thee alone do I trust, for Thou art Almighty and infinitely Good, and know my weakness, and my proneness to yield myself up a willing captive to my enemies, unless Thou help me. Help me, therefore, my Hope, and the Strength of my soul!"

It is a virtual request, when we lift up our heart to God to gain some grace, showing Him our need without molding our thoughts into words or sentences. When, for instance, I lift up my mind to God, and present before Him the consciousness of my own inability either to defend myself from any evil, or to perform any good action; and burning in His presence with the desire to serve Him, I humbly and faithfully await His help, and admire and intently gaze upon the Lord Himself.

This confession of our weakness, enkindled with fervent desire and faith towards God, is a prayer which virtually asks for what I want; and the more convinced we are of our weakness when we acknowledge it, and the more ardent our desire, and the more vivid our faith, the more efficacious will our prayer be.

There is another and more swift kind of virtual prayer, which consists of a mere glance of the mind towards God, so as to implore His help, which glance is, as it were, a silent remembrancer, asking for the grace which we had before prayed for.

We should strive to form the habit of praying in this way, for it is a weapon of more value and assistance than I can say (as experience has shown), and one which we may lay hold of at all times and on all occasions.

CHAPTER 46

Of Meditation.

IF you wish to spend some time in prayer—half an hour, or an hour, or more—you will do well to make a meditation on the Life and Passion of Jesus Christ, and in it always apply His actions to the particular virtue which you are seeking to gain.

Thus, if you are seeking to obtain patience, you would select for your subject of meditation the Mystery of the Scourging.

Consider, first, how after the command was given by Pilate, our Lord was dragged with scoffs and cries, by wicked men, to the place appointed for His Scourging.

Secondly, think how He was stripped by them with impatient fury of His garments, so that His most Pure Flesh was left naked and exposed.

Thirdly, consider how His innocent Hands were tightly bound with hard cords, and fastened to the pillar.

Fourthly, consider how His whole Body was torn and gashed with blows, so that His Divine Blood in streams ran down to the ground.

Fifthly, see repeated lashes fall upon the same place, exasperating the wounds already made.

Whilst you dwell upon these, or similar points of consideration, in order to gain patience, first apply your senses to feel, in the highest degree possible, the intense agony and acute suffering which your dear Lord endured in every part of His most Sacred Body, and throughout all of it at once.

Then pass to His interior Sufferings, and strive to enter into the meekness and patience with which He bore so great agonies in His most Holy Soul, and consider how, unsatisfied with these, He hungered to suffer even more excruciating sufferings for the glory of His Father and for our good.

Then see Him inflamed with the fervent desire that you should willingly bear your affliction, and still turning to His Father, behold Him praying for you, that He would vouchsafe to give you grace patiently to bear your cross, both that which is now weighing heavily upon you, and all others which may be laid upon you hereafter.

Here bend your will again and again to will to suffer all with a patient spirit; and then, turning to the Eternal Father, thank Him for having, out of His pure Love, sent His Only-begotten Son into the world to endure such bitter pain, and to intercede for you; then ask Him through the merit of the Works and Prayers of His Beloved Son, to grant you the virtue of patience.

CHAPTER 47

Of another Way of Praying by Way of Meditation.

YOU may also resort to another plan of praying and meditating. After you have attentively considered the afflictions of the Lord, and dwelt upon His cheerful acceptance of them, you may pass on from the greatness of His Travail and of His Patience to two other considerations:

The one, of His Merit; the other, of the Satisfaction and Glory which the Eternal Father derived from the perfect obedience of His Son in His Passion.

And bringing both of these things before His Divine Majesty, ask through their virtue the grace which you desire.

And this you may do, not only in each Mystery of our Lord's Passion, but in each separate act, whether interior or exterior, in each Mystery.

CHAPTER 48

Of a Way of Praying by means of the Blessed Virgin Mary.

BESIDES the modes of meditating already referred to, there is another way of meditating, which has reference to the Blessed Virgin Mary. First, turn your thoughts to the Eternal Father, next address yourself to the sweet and beloved Jesus, and lastly, contemplate His ever-blessed Mother.

Whilst turning to God the Father, consider two things; first, His delight in beholding from all eternity Mary, before He had drawn her out of nothingness; secondly, the graces and virtues she displayed, after God sent her into the world.

Enter into the first point thus:

Begin by raising your thoughts above all created things; go back into the eternity which preceded all creation, enter into the mind of God, and see what delight He took in the thought of the Virgin Mary; ask Him, by that delight, for the grace and strength you need for conquering your enemies, and particularly that one against which you are now struggling.

Then consider the great and singular virtues and actions of the most holy Mother, bring all and each before God, asking Him by the grace which He wrought in her, that He would of His Divine Goodness grant you what you require.

Then turn to God the Son, and remind Him of the virginal womb in which He was borne for nine months, of the adoration which, after He was born, the Blessed Virgin paid Him, recognizing Him at once as God and man, as her Son and her Creator; of the compassionate gaze with which she contemplated Him in His poverty; of the arms which embraced Him; of the loving kisses with which she caressed Him; of the breasts which fed Him; of the pain and anguish she endured for His sake throughout His Life, and at His Death. By these memories you will bring to bear a sweet pressure upon the Divine Son, Who is ever ready to hear your prayer.

Lastly, contemplate the most Holy Virgin herself, remembering how Divine Providence from all eternity has chosen her to be the Mother of the Author of grace and pity, so that, beneath her Blessed Son, there is no one so full of tenderness, no one whose prayers are so powerful. Represent that which has been written of her, and which it is said experience has found by so many wonderful results, that no one ever faithfully asked that her prayers might be granted to them, and asked in vain. Recall the sufferings which her Son endured for your salvation; ask that her prayers may obtain grace for you to profit by them, that His Passion may work in you the results He desired, to His glory and Satisfaction.

CHAPTER 49

Of certain Considerations as to Faith and Confidence in the Prayers of the Virgin Mary.

IF you would have recourse to the prayers of the Blessed Virgin with confidence, you may encourage yourself by the following considerations.

First, every one knows by experience that a vessel which has contained musk or any other precious perfume, retains the odor of it after it has been removed; and the longer the perfume has been in the vessel, the longer does the fragrance linger about it, and this is more the case when some of the liquid itself still remains. But the virtue of the musk, or of any other perfume, is limited and finite.

Now, if this be so, with what a glow of charity, with what a richness of tenderness and pity, must the heart of Mary have been kindled and filled! For nine months did she carry in her virginal womb Him Who is essentially Love, Mercy and Pity, and Who in an infinite manner possessed those attributes; and still in her heart and love does He ever abide. If he who comes near to a great fire cannot but feel a portion of its heat; much more, shall we not, as we contemplate that fire of charity, mercy and pity which glowed in Mary, be conscious of some effluence of its rays, enkindling and elevating our spiritual life; and this the more, the oftener we draw near, and the greater the faith and confidence with which we ask that her prayers may be granted to us.

Secondly, no created being ever loved Jesus Christ so ardently as she did, nor was there ever any one who was so perfectly conformed to His Will as His most holy Mother.

If then the Son of God, Who gave His whole Life and Himself for us, to redeem us from our sins, has made His Mother in a way to become the mother of all who share His nature, that she beneath Himself may have our interests at heart, and that she may aid us with her prayers, how can we doubt, if this be so, but that she fulfils His purposes in her with regard to us?

Therefore we may confidently ask that her prayers may be vouchsafed to us in all our needs, for this belief is very blessed; as she may obtain for us many gifts of grace and mercy.

CHAPTER 50

Of a Way of Meditating and Praying by means of the Angels and of all the Blessed.

THERE are two ways of dealing with the Saints and Angels in Heaven in order to obtain their assistance.

The first is, to represent to the Eternal Father the praises and glory which He receives from the heavenly Court, and also to bring before Him the toils and pains which the Saints have suffered on earth for His love; and by virtue of these to ask of His Divine Majesty all that we need.

The second is, to ask for the prayers of those glorious spirits, who not only desire our perfection, but also that we may be in a far higher position than they are; begging that they may aid you against every enemy and every form of sin, and especially may guard you in the hour of death.

At other times you will reflect upon the many and singular graces which they have received from their Sovereign Creator, kindling in yourself lively affections of love and joy for those precious gifts with which they are enriched, rejoicing as if all those gifts had been bestowed upon yourself.

You should carry this disinterested joy even to a greater pitch than this, and even, if possible, rejoice that they rather than yourself have been thus favored, since it is God's Will; and render, therefore, to Him thanks and praise.

To practice this devotion with ease and order, you may divide the different orders of the Blessed into seven parts, according to the seven days of the week.

Thus: on Sunday, honor the nine choirs of the Angels; on Monday, St. John the Baptist; on Tuesday, the Patriarchs and Prophets; on Wednesday, the Apostles; on Thursday, the Martyrs; on Friday, Bishops and other Saints; and on Saturday, the Virgins and other Saints.

But omit not on any day the Blessed Virgin, Queen of all Saints; your guardian Angel; St. Michael, the Archangel; and all your patrons.

Daily entreat the Eternal Father and His Beloved Son, and ask for the prayers of the Blessed Virgin, that St. Joseph, the spouse of the Blessed Virgin, may also aid you, and confidently ask God for his special care and protection. Many wonderful things are told us of this glorious Saint, and of the many favors, both temporal and spiritual, which have been granted to those who have honored him with pious veneration, and devoutly sought his prayers—more especially to those who have wanted help in prayer and meditation.

For if God has so greatly honored other saints who during their life have rendered honor and service to Him, what esteem will He have for that most humble and blessed Saint, whom He Himself so honored upon earth as to be subject to him as to a father, and so obeyed and served him!

CHAPTER 51

Of Meditation on the Passion of Christ, with a view to excite various Affections.

WHAT has already been said respecting meditation on the Lord's Passion, relates to that manner of praying which consists in seeking something from God. I am going now to refer to it, in order to show how we may in this way excite divers affections.

I will imagine, then, that you have chosen the Crucifixion for your meditation. In this Mystery you may dwell on the following points among others:

First, consider how the furious people on Mount Calvary passionately stripped our Lord; and how His Flesh, through the Scourging He endured, stuck to His clothes, and was torn off in pieces.

Secondly, how the crown of thorns was taken off His Head, and again pressed upon It, so that the thorns were driven in again.

Thirdly, how with the blows of the hammer and with nails, He was cruelly fastened to the Cross.

Fourthly, how, when His sacred Limbs would not reach the places where the holes were made to receive the nails, those savage dogs stretched his Arms and Legs so violently that His disjointed Bones might be numbered.

Fifthly, how, as the Lord hung on the hard wood of the Cross, the weight of His Body in that position increased the size of His most Sacred Wounds, and aggravated inexpressibly the pain.

In order to excite in yourself, by these and other considerations of the same kind, the affection of love, strive to gain more and more deeply the knowledge of your Lord's Infinite Goodness and Love towards you, Who for your sake willed to suffer such cruel torments; for the more you advance in this knowledge, the more will you increase in love.

This knowledge, too, of the Goodness and Infinite Love of your Lord, will excite in you contrition and regret for having so often and so ungratefully offended a God Who was for your sins in so many ways ill-treated and tortured.

To call out hope, consider, that into this state of misery your mighty Lord descended, that He might destroy sin, and rescue you from the snares of the devil, and from the faults which you have committed; that He might reconcile you to His Eternal Father, and give you boldness to draw near to Him in every need.

To call out joy, pass from the consideration of the Passion to the thought of its results; you will see how this Passion has the power of purifying the whole world from sin, and of satisfying Divine Justice; how it has confounded the Prince of darkness, vanquished death, and filled again the void places in the angelic ranks.

Joy will be heightened by the consideration of the joy of the Most Holy Trinity, of the Blessed Virgin, of the Church Militant and Triumphant, in these results.

To excite in yourself a hatred for your own sins, bring the points of meditation to bear upon yourself, by regarding the Passion of the Savior as endured for no other end than to inspire you with hatred for your evil inclinations, and especially for the one which most of all has dominion over you, and which is most displeasing to the Divine Goodness.

To move you to wonder, consider what greater marvel could there be than to behold the Creator of the universe, Who imparts life to all, persecuted to death by His own creatures: to see Supreme Majesty trampled upon and despised; to behold Justice condemned; to see Divine Beauty spit upon; the Love of the Heavenly Father hated; the inner and unapproachable Light brought under the power of darkness; Essential Blessedness and Glory reckoned as the dishonor and disgrace of the human race, and overwhelmed in abject misery.

To stir in yourself the feeling of compassion for your Suffering Lord, besides meditating on the pains of His Body, strive to enter into those incomparably greater sufferings which He endured in His Soul. For if you are capable of being touched by the former, it will be wonderful if your heart is not broken by the thought of the latter.

The Soul of Christ beheld the Divinity, as It now beholds It in Heaven; He knew It, then, to be infinitely worthy of all honor and worship, and through the unspeakable Love with which this knowledge inspired Him for It, He burnt with the desire that all creatures should devote themselves with all their powers to the Divine Majesty.

To see the Divine Essence, then, so strangely outraged and despised by the innumerable faults and abominable sins of the world, pierced Him through and through with darts of sorrow, which tortured Him in proportion to the greatness of His Love, and the intensity of His desire that all men should honor and obey so exalted a Majesty.

As we cannot measure the greatness of this love and desire, even so can we not estimate how bitter and grievous was the inward sorrow of our Crucified Lord on that account.

His love for all creatures, a love unspeakable, was another ground of sorrow; in proportion to His love for them, did He grieve intensely for all their sins, which separated them from Him. He grieved for every mortal sin which had been, or which ever should be, committed by all men who had lived, or hereafter should live, upon the earth; for every mortal sin separates the soul of the sinner from the Soul of the Lord, to which by charity it was united.

Such a separation is far more painful than dismemberment of the body; inasmuch as the soul, being altogether spiritual, and of a nature more noble and perfect than the body, is therefore more capable of suffering.

Yet of all the sorrows which our Lord endured for His creatures, the most bitter was that which He felt for the sins of the damned, who, as they could not again be united to Him, would have to suffer torments eternal and inconceivable.

And if the soul, already touched with the view of these sufferings of her Beloved Jesus, would penetrate more deeply into them, it would be found that there was ample cause for compassion, in the heavy grief He endured, not only for sins actually committed, but also for all possible forms of sins; for doubtless it is to His Passion we are indebted both for the pardon of the former, and for preservation from the latter, both having been purchased for us by His precious Sufferings.

Nor will other considerations be wanting, beloved, to move you to sympathize with the Crucified; for there never was a grief, and never will be one, endured by any reasonable being, which He Himself has not tasted. Injuries, reproaches, temptations, pains, mortifications, and every grief and trouble which the human race can know, pierced more keenly the Soul of Christ than the souls of those who actually suffer them.

For every separate suffering, great or small, of body or of mind, even to a slight headache or a prick of a needle, was clearly seen by our most Pitiful Lord, who of His boundless love was pleased to compassionate them and to engrave them on His Heart.

But who can express what He felt at the sight of the sorrows of His most holy Mother? For in every respect and in every way in which the Lord sorrowed and suffered, did the Holy Virgin sorrow and suffer, not with equal intensity, but most bitterly nevertheless.

And these her sorrows opened anew the inward wounds of her Blessed Son. These, like so many fiery darts of love, pierced His most loving Heart, which by reason of all the torments which have been mentioned, and of others unknown—yet infinite in number—which He endured, may be well described in the words of a devout soul, who in holy simplicity was wont to call it "a loving hell of voluntary sufferings."

Consider then, beloved, the cause of all this anguish, borne by our Crucified Redeemer and Lord, and you will find that it is nothing else but sin; therefore the genuine and principal way of showing the sympathy and gratitude which He demands of us, and which we are undoubtedly bound to render to Him, is to be sorry for our past sins purely from love to Him; to hate sin with a hatred beyond all other hatred, and to fight manfully against all His enemies and our own evil inclinations; that thus, putting off the old man with his deeds, we may be clothed with the new, and our souls may be adorned with the virtues of the Christian character.

CHAPTER 52

Of the Advantages which may be derived from Meditation on the
Crucifixion of our Lord, and the Imitation of His Virtues.

AMONG the many benefits which may be obtained by holy meditation, the first is, not only sorrow for past sin, but also regret for the disorderly passions which are still alive within you, and which nailed your Lord to the Cross.

The second is, to seek pardon of your sins, and the grace of a perfect hatred of yourself, that you may never more offend Him; but, in return for all His sufferings for you, love and serve Him with all your heart, which is simply impossible, without a holy hatred of self.

The third is, the resolve to attack and uproot all your evil propensities, however trifling they may appear.

The fourth is, the effort to imitate with all your might the virtues of the Savior, Who suffered not only to redeem us and make satisfaction for our sins, but also to leave us an example that we should follow His holy steps.

Here I will suggest a plan of meditation which may serve for this purpose.

Suppose, for example, you are seeking to form patience; in imitating Christ your Lord, take the following points.

First, consider how the Soul of Christ in the Passion acted towards God.

Secondly, how God acted towards the Soul of Christ.

Thirdly, how the Soul of Christ acted towards Itself, and towards His most holy Body.

Fourthly, how Christ acted towards us.

Fifthly, how we should act towards Christ.

First, consider how the Soul of Christ, gazing intently upon God, marveled to behold that infinite, incomprehensible Greatness—in comparison with which all created things are as a mere nothing—treated with the greatest indignity on earth (yet still abiding changeless in Its Glory), and this for man, from whom It has received no return but that of unfaithfulness and insult; consider how His Soul adored God, gave Him thanks, and offered Itself wholly to Him.

Secondly, see how God Himself acted towards the Soul of Christ; how He willed and moved It to endure for our sake buffetings, spittings, blasphemies, scourgings, thorns, and at last the Cross, revealing to It all the satisfaction which He felt in seeing It laden with every kind of affliction and ignominy.

Thirdly, pass to the consideration of the Soul of Christ in reference to Itself. Think how His understanding, which is all Light, perceived how great this good pleasure of God was in seeing Him suffer; and how with Its affection, which is all Fire, It loved His Divine Majesty with unbounded love, because of His infinite Excellence and Its infinite indebtedness to Him. Think also how, being thus called by Him to suffer for our sake and for our example, His will contentedly and joyfully accepted and obeyed with readiness the Divine appointment. And who can penetrate the deep longings of that most pure and loving Soul thus to suffer? It dwelt, as it were, in a labyrinth of sorrows, ever seeking new modes of suffering, and never (as It would) satisfying the desire. It gave Itself freely and wholly, and Its most innocent Flesh, as a prey to wicked men and infernal spirits, to be dealt with as they pleased.

Fourthly, then contemplate your Savior, as He turns His pitying Eyes on you, and says, "Behold, My child, whither your immoderate desires have carried Me, because you would not do a little violence to yourself. Behold how much, and how gladly, have I suffered for love of you, and to set you an example of true patience. By all My sorrows, I beseech you, beloved child, to bear this cross willingly, and every other you may yet have to bear according to My good pleasure; surrendering yourself into the hands of all your persecutors, whom I may permit to molest you, however vile they may be, and fierce against your reputation or your body. Oh! didst thou but know the comfort of acting thus! These Wounds bear testimony to this truth, which I was pleased to receive as costly gems, so that I might adorn with precious virtues that poor soul of thine—dear to Me beyond thy conception. And if on this account I am brought to such an extremity, wilt thou, beloved spouse, refuse to suffer a little in order to satisfy My Heart, and allay the anguish of those Wounds which thy impatience has inflicted, which grieves Me far more bitterly than the Wounds themselves?"

Fifthly, next consider Who it is that thus holds converse with you, and you will see that it is Christ Himself, the King of Glory, Very God and Very Man. Consider the greatness of His sufferings and His ignominy, which would have exceeded the deserts of the lowest criminal in the world. Behold your Lord, not only preserving calmness, and marvelously patient, but rejoicing as at His nuptials; and as a little water sprinkled on a fire serves but to quicken the flame, so with the increase of His agonies, which to His overflowing Love seemed little, did His joy increase, and His eager desire to suffer still more. Bear in mind, too, that your most merciful Lord did and suffered all this, not from necessity nor for any advantage to Himself, but (as He has told you) from the motive of love for you, and in order that you might have His example to help you in gaining the virtue of patience. Endeavor, then, to acquire a perfect knowledge of what He desires of you, and of the delight He takes in seeing you exercise yourself in this virtue. Make acts of ardent desire to bear, not only without complaint, but even with joy, your present cross and all others which may be your lot, even if they are heavier, that you may become more like your God, and give Him greater comfort. Picture to yourself the shame and bitterness He endured for your sake, and His steadfastness and patience; and then, avow to your shame that your patience is hardly to be called a shadow of His, and that your sorrows and humiliation are imaginary. And fear and tremble, lest for a moment the slightest feeling of reluctance to suffer for love of your Lord be permitted to find the least resting-place in your heart.

This Crucified Lord, beloved, is the book which I put into your hands, and by reading It you may learn the true form of every virtue.

It is the Book of Life, which not only by means of words enlightens the understanding, but also by Its living Example enkindles the will.

The world is full of books; and yet, were they all put together, they could not teach so perfectly how to gain all virtues, as does the contemplation of a Crucified God.

There are, however, some who spend whole hours in weeping over our Lord's Passion, and meditating on His patience; and yet, when troubles arise, they manifest as much impatience, as if in prayer they had learnt quite another lesson.

Such persons are like those soldiers, who in their tents, before battle, are full of heroism, but when the fight really begins, cast away their arms and take to flight. Can any thing be more sad and foolish, than to contemplate as in a mirror the Virtues of the Lord, to be enamored of them, and to admire them, and then, when an opportunity offers itself of exercising them, entirely to forget and neglect them?

CHAPTER 53

Of the most Holy Sacrament of the Eucharist.

THUS far, beloved, I have provided you with four weapons, which are necessary for you in order to overcome your enemies; and I have also given you directions how to manage them effectively.

There yet remains another, of which I ought to treat, namely, the most holy Sacrament of the Eucharist.

And inasmuch as this Sacrament is above all others, so this fifth weapon surpasses all the rest.

The four of which I have spoken draw their virtue from the Merits and grace purchased for us by the Blood of Christ, but this weapon is itself the very Flesh and Blood together with the Soul and Divinity of Christ.

With regard to the four first weapons, we fight against our enemies in the strength of Christ, but in this fifth one, we fight against them with Christ Himself; and Christ Himself fights against them with us. For whoso eats the Flesh of Christ and drinks His Blood, dwells in Christ, and Christ in him.

This weapon, the most holy Sacrament, may be taken in two ways, namely, sacramentally and spiritually: in the former, it may be daily; in the latter, every hour and every moment. You must not then neglect to receive It very often in the second way, and always when you are permitted in the first.

CHAPTER 54

Of the Way we ought to Receive the most Holy Sacrament of the Eucharist.

THERE are many ends which we may propose to ourselves in approaching this most divine Sacrament, to attain which we have several things to do at three different times: namely, before Communion, when Communicating, and after Communion.

Whatever end we have in view in communicating, we must cleanse and purify our soul, in the sacrament of Repentance, if defiled with the guilt of mortal sin. After this we must offer ourselves with our whole heart, and our whole soul, and our whole strength, and our whole powers, without reserve, to Jesus Christ and to His good pleasure, since in this most holy Sacrament He gives us His Blood and His Flesh, with His Soul, His Divinity, and His Merits. And, with the consciousness that our gift is so narrow, nay nothing, when compared with His, we should desire to possess, and to present to His Divine Majesty, all that has been, or ever will be, offered and given to Him by all creatures, on earth and in Heaven.

If your intention in communicating be to obtain some victory over your enemies and His, and to destroy them, begin, in this case, on the eve of your Communion, or before, to meditate on the desire of the Son of God to enter into your heart, and to unite Himself to you, and to help you to overcome your evil passions.

This desire is so intense and so boundless in Christ, that a created intellect is unable to comprehend it.

But that you may in some measure approach a just idea of it, there are two things which must be impressed on your mind. One is the unspeakable pleasure which God in His Goodness takes in dwelling with us; for He calls it His delight.

The other, His infinite hatred of sin, both as a bar and hindrance to His union with us, which He so much desires; and because of its utter opposition to His Divine Perfections. For being Himself the Sovereign Good, Pure Light, and Infinite Beauty, He cannot but infinitely abhor and detest sin, which is nothing but darkness, defect, and an insufferable deformity of our souls.

So burning, indeed, is the hatred of the Lord against sin, that all that He has wrought both in the Old Testament and in the New had for its end the destruction of sin; above all, the most holy Passion of His Son, Who (as some of God's enlightened servants have said) would, if needful, expose Himself anew to a thousand deaths, to destroy in us every fault, even the smallest.

These reflections will aid you to form an idea, however imperfectly, of the intensity with which the Lord desires to enter into your heart, in order that He might drive out and exterminate every enemy both of Himself and of you; and thus will you yourself be stirred up with a lively desire to receive Him, for the same object.

The hope of the arrival of our Heavenly Captain will encourage and inspirit us to challenge repeatedly the passion which we have set ourselves to overcome, and to repress it by a constant and deadly opposition, and to make acts of the contrary virtue; and this you should continue to do, both on the evening and morning before the most Holy Communion.

Then, when we are on the point of Communicating, review for a moment all the faults of which, since your last Communion, you have been guilty, as though God did not exist, or as if He had not endured so much for you in the Mysteries of the Cross; how you have preferred a trifling pleasure and the gratification of your own desires to the Will of God and His Honor; and thus with holy fear you will be ashamed at the sight of your ingratitude and unworthiness. But consider, again, how the boundless deep of your Lord's Goodness calls to the deep of your ingratitude and unfaithfulness, and approach Him with trustfulness, giving Him a large place in your heart, that He may take absolute possession of it.

And you will be able to do this, as soon as you have driven out of your heart all attachment to creatures, closing it against them, that your Lord may enter it alone.

After Communion, withdraw at once into the inner sanctuary of your heart, and having first adored Him, then with all lowliness and reverence converse thus in spirit with your Lord: "Thou see, O my only Good, how prone I am to offend Thee, and what power this passion exercises over me, and how in my own strength I cannot free myself from it. This conflict, then, is chiefly Thine, and it is from Thee alone I can hope for victory, though I must do my part."

Then turn to the Eternal Father, and offer to Him His Blessed Son, Whom He has given to you, and Whom you now possess within you, as a thank-offering and for victory over yourself. Then, make a vigorous attack upon the passion, and wait in faith upon God for the victory, Who will (though for awhile He may seem to delay) never fail you, if you, on your side, make every possible effort.

CHAPTER 55

How we ought to Prepare ourselves for Communion in order to excite within us Love.

IN order to stir up within you the love of God, by means of this most Heavenly Sacrament, let your meditation on the preceding evening be upon His Love for you.

You should consider how that Great and Almighty Lord, not content with having made you after His own image and likeness, and with having sent His Only-begotten Son on earth to suffer during three and thirty years for your sins, and to endure the most bitter sorrows and the painful death of the Cross for your redemption, was, besides all this, pleased to leave Him with you for your food and support in the most holy Sacrament of the Altar.

Weigh well, beloved, the singular greatness of this Love, which, viewed on every side, is most perfect and matchless:

First, if we regard its duration, our God has loved us unceasingly and from all eternity; as by His Divinity He is Eternal, so His Love is Eternal, whereby, before all worlds, He decreed in His Heart to give us His Son in this wonderful manner.

Rejoicing at this thought, say to yourself with inward joy, "In those depths of eternity, my insignificant being was then so loved and esteemed by the Most High God, that He thought of me, and designed in His unspeakable Love to give me His Own Son for my food."

Secondly, all other love, however great it may be, has a bound which it cannot pass, but the Love of our Lord is alone without measure.

Desiring, therefore, to fully satisfy it, He has given His Dear Son, co-equal to Himself in Majesty and Infinity, of One and the Same Substance and Nature. Thus the Love is equal to the Gift, and the Gift to the Love; and both are so great, that nothing greater can be conceived by the human mind.

Thirdly, God was not drawn to love us through any necessity or constraint, but His Own Intrinsic and Natural Goodness alone moved Him to love us with so great and so incomprehensible an affection.

Fourthly, no work of ours or merit could have preceded this love, so as to induce this mighty Lord to show such amazing love towards our baseness; but it must be owing to His free Bounty alone that He has given Himself wholly and entirely to us, His most unworthy creatures.

Fifthly, if you direct your thoughts to the purity of this love, you will see that it is not, like the world's love, mixed with any self-interest. For the Lord has no need of our goods, being, without us, in Himself Alone most Blessed and most Glorious; and He sheds forth His unspeakable Love and Beneficence upon us simply for our benefit, and not for His.

Consider well this truth, and you will say in your heart, "How is it that a God so Great sets His Heart on so vile a creature? What could be Thy design, O King of Glory? What dost Thou look for from me, who am but a little dust? I see well, O my God, by the light of Thy burning Charity, that Thou hast but one design, which reveals to me most plainly the disinterestedness of Thy love for me; for Thou dost give me Thy Whole Self to be my Food, for no other purpose than that I should be wholly changed into Thee. And this Thou doest, not that Thou hast any need of me, but that, Thou living in me and I in Thee, I may by a loving union be changed into Thee, and my earthly heart be made with Thee a heart only Divine."

Then, filled with wonder and joy at the thought of God's high esteem and love for you, and knowing that He, by His Almighty Love, seeks and desires only to draw your whole heart to Himself, detach yourself from all creatures, and from yourself also as one of them, and offer yourself without reserve as a whole burnt-offering to your Lord, that His Love and His Divine pleasure may henceforth guide your understanding, your will, and your memory, and may regulate all your senses.

Then, perceiving that nothing is so calculated to work in you these Divine effects, as a worthy reception of the most holy Sacrament of the Altar, open your heart for this purpose with the following ejaculations and loving aspirations:

"O most Heavenly Food, when will the hour come when I shall wholly sacrifice myself to Thee in the fire of Thy Love? When, when? O Love uncreated!"

"O living Bread, when shall I live by Thee alone, for Thee alone, and to Thee alone? Oh! when, my Life? Blessed Life, Beautiful and Eternal?"

"O Heavenly Manna! When shall I loathe all other earthly food, and crave for Thee alone—feed on Thee alone? When shall this be, O my Sweetness, when, my only Good? O my Loving and Almighty Lord, deliver now my wretched heart from every attachment, and from every evil passion; adorn it with Thy holy virtues, and with a pure intention of doing all things solely to please Thee; that so I may open my heart to Thee, invite Thee, and with a sweet violence constrain Thee to come in, that Thou, O Lord, may then work in me, without resistance, all that Thou hast ever desired to effect."

With such loving affections, you should exercise yourself in the evening and morning before Communion. Then, as the time of Communion draws near, consider what you are about to take; no less than the Son of God, of Majesty Incomprehensible, before Whom the Heavens and all the powers therein do tremble—the Holy of Holies, the Spotless Mirror, and the incomprehensible Purity, in comparison with Whom no creature is clean; the One Who, as a worm and an outcast of the people, willed for love of you to be rejected, trampled upon, mocked, spit upon, and crucified, by the malice and wickedness of the world. You are about to receive God, in Whose Hands are the life and death of the whole universe.

Then, on the other hand, regard yourself; think how you are nothing, and that by your sins and wickedness you have made yourself lower than the vilest and foulest of the irrational creatures, and that you have rendered yourself worthy to be the sport and mockery of all the devils in hell; how, instead of being grateful for such great and numberless benefits, you have in your capriciousness and willfulness despised this so Mighty and so Loving a Lord, and trampled under foot His Precious Blood.

Yet, notwithstanding all this, His Love abides, His Goodness is unchanged, He still invites you to His Divine Banquet; nay, He even constrains you to come to it, threatening you with death if you refuse His invitation. He shuts not the door of His Mercy, nor turns His back upon you, though by nature you have become leprous, lame, dropsical, blind, possessed by devils, and have 'gone after many lovers.'

He asks this of you and no more:

First, to mourn for your offences against Him.

Second, to hate above all things sin, both great and small.

Thirdly, to offer and give yourself wholly to do His Will and Bidding, ever with affection, and with action, when opportunity presents.

Fourthly, to have faith and firm hope that He will forgive you, and cleanse you from your sins, and defend you from all your enemies.

Fortified by this unspeakable Love of the Lord, you will draw near to communicate, with a holy and loving fear, saying: "Lord, I am not worthy to receive Thee, because I have so many, many times grievously offended Thee, nor have I yet mourned as much as I should, over the offences which I have committed against Thee."

"Lord, I am not worthy to receive Thee, because I am not yet entirely free from affection to venial sins."

"Lord, I am not worthy to receive Thee, for I have not yet wholly yielded myself up to Thy Love, Thy Will, and Thy Bidding."

"O my Almighty Lord, infinitely Good, for the sake of Thy Goodness and Thy Word, make me worthy, O my Love, with this faith to receive Thee."

When you have communicated, shut yourself up immediately in the secret recess of your heart, and setting aside all created things, hold converse with your Lord in some such form as the following: "O Most High King of Heaven, what has brought Thee to me, who am miserable, poor, blind, and naked?" And He will answer you—"Love."

And you will reply to Him, "O uncreated Love, sweet Love, what wilt Thou that I should give Thee?"

And He will answer "only Love." "I will that no other fire should burn upon the altar of your heart, and in your sacrifices, and in all your works, but the fire of My Love, which, consuming all other love, and all self-will, will rise to Me as the sweetest odor.

"This is what I have continually sought from you, and still seek, because I desire to be wholly thine, and that you should be wholly Mine; but such a union cannot be, till, having surrendered yourself entirely, which it is My great delight that you should do, you are delivered from all love of self, all love of your own opinion, all love of your own will and reputation."

"I seek from you hatred of yourself, and I will give you in exchange My Love; I ask for your heart, that it may be united to Mine, for to this end was Mine pierced upon the Cross; I ask you to give Me yourself without reserve, that I may be wholly yours."

"You see that I am of infinite value; yet of My Goodness I estimate myself at your value. Buy Me then now, beloved, by giving yourself for Me."

"I desire this of you, beloved, that you should have no other will than Mine, that all your thoughts, your aims, your desires, should be of Me and according to My Will, that I may will, think, intend, and see all that you will, think, intend, and see; so that your nothingness may be swallowed up in the depth of My infinity, and transformed into it. Thus will you be fully blest and happy in Me, and I completely contented in you."

In conclusion, offer to the Father His only Son, first, for a thank-offering; then for your own needs, and those of all the Holy Church, and for all who belong to you, and to whom you are in any way bound, and for the souls who are being cleansed from the remaining stains of sins; and make this offering in commemoration of, and in union with, that which He made of Himself, when He offered Himself to the Father, hanging upon the Cross, and covered with blood.

And you may likewise unite your offering with all the sacrifices offered on that day in the Holy Catholic Church.

CHAPTER 56

Of Spiritual Communion.

ALTHOUGH we may not receive the Lord sacramentally more than once a day, yet we may, as I have before remarked, receive Him spiritually every hour, and every moment; and nothing but negligence or some other fault on our part can deprive us of this privilege.

Spiritual Communion may even be more advantageous to us and acceptable to God than many Sacramental Communions, when the latter are received with imperfect dispositions.

As often then as you shall dispose yourself and prepare for spiritual Communion, you will find the Son of God ready to give Himself with His Own Hands to you for your spiritual food.

By way of preparation, turn your thoughts to Him for this end; and after a short examination of your failings, mourn with Him over your offences, and with all humility and faith beseech Him that He would vouchsafe to enter into your poor soul with some fresh gift of grace, to heal it and fortify it against the enemy.

When about to do violence to yourself and to mortify some appetite, or to do some act of virtue, do all with the motive of preparing your heart for your Lord, Who is continually demanding this of you; and then turn to Him and invite Him with earnestness to come with His Grace to heal you and deliver you from your enemies, to the end that He Alone may possess your heart. Or else, calling to mind your last Sacramental Communion, say with enkindled heart, "When, my Lord, shall I again receive Thee?—when? when?"

But if you desire to prepare yourself, and spiritually communicate in a more orderly manner; on the previous evening address all mortifications, acts of virtue, and every other good work to this end, that you may spiritually receive your Lord.

And in the early morning, consider what great happiness and benefit the soul gains by worthily receiving the most holy Sacrament of the Altar (for in it lost virtue is regained, the soul is brought back to its first beauty and receives the fruits and merits of the Passion of the Son of God); and consider how pleasing it is to God, that we receive it and possess these blessings, so that you may inflame your heart with a great desire to receive it to give Him pleasure.

When this desire is enkindled within you, turning to Him, say: "Inasmuch as it is not granted to me, Lord, today to receive Thee Sacramentally, grant, O uncreated Goodness and Power, that I—every fault having been pardoned and healed—may now worthily receive Thee spiritually, every hour and every day, and provide me with fresh grace and strength against all my enemies, and particularly against that one, upon whom, for Thy pleasure, I am making war."

CHAPTER 57

Of returning Thanks.

SINCE all the good we have or do, is of God, and from God, we are bound to render thanks for all our virtuous exercises and victories, and for every benefit, particular and general, which we have received from His Pitiful Hand.

And to do this in a proper manner, we must consider the end for which our Lord is moved to communicate His grace to us; for, from this consideration and knowledge, we come to learn how God wills that we should return thanks.

And since in every benefit the Lord principally intends His own Honor, and to draw us to His love and service, first think with yourself in this way: "With what power, wisdom, and goodness, has my God granted and given to me this blessing and grace!"

Then, seeing that in you (as of yourself) there is nothing which could merit any blessing, but on the contrary nothing else but demerit and ingratitude, with profound humility address your Lord: "How is it, O Lord, that Thou deign to regard a dead dog, bestowing so many benefits upon me? May Thy Name be blessed for ever and ever!"

And lastly, seeing that by the benefit He seeks again to be loved and served by you, inflame yourself with love towards so loving a Lord, and with sincere desire to serve Him in His way. And therefore to this end you will add a full offering of yourself, such as may be made in the following manner.

CHAPTER 58

Of Oblation.

TO the end that the oblation of yourself may be on all sides pleasing to God, two things are necessary. One is, union with the offerings which Christ made to the Father; the other is, that your will be detached from all irregular affection for the creature.

By the first thing, you must know that the Son of God, when living in this vale of tears, offered to His Heavenly Father not only Himself and His works, but with Himself us also and our works.

So that our offerings must be made in union with, and trustful dependence upon His.

For the second thing, consider well before you make your offering, whether your will has any attachment, for if so, it must first be disengaged from every affection; and have recourse to God, in order that He, with His right Hand, may loose you; so that, freed and delivered from all hindrance, you may be able to offer yourself to His Divine Majesty.

And be very watchful on this point; since, if you offer yourself to God, whilst some irregular affection for the creature remains, you do not offer yourself, but that which is another's, in that you are not your own, but belong to those creatures to whom your heart is given; a thing which is displeasing to the Lord—as if it were your desire to mock Him. Hence it is, that so many oblations of ourselves not only return to us void and fruitless, but afterwards we fall into various defects and sins.

We may offer ourselves to God, whilst still cleaving to the creatures, but it must be in order that by His Goodness we may be set free, so that we may be able to offer ourselves wholly to His Divine Majesty, and to His service; and this we should do often, and with great affection.

Let then your offering be without attachment, and without regard to your own desires, not aiming at earthly blessings or Heavenly, but purely at the Will and Providence of God, to which you ought entirely to submit, and to sacrifice yourself as a perpetual burnt-offering, and, weaned from all created things, say: "Behold, my Lord and Creator, each and every desire of mine is at the disposal of Thy Will and Eternal Providence; do with me as it pleases Thee, in life, in death, and after death; in time, and in eternity."

If you act thus in sincerity (which will be proved when some adversity arises) you will become from an earthly, a dealer in Heavenly and most blessed goods, for you shall be God's, and God shall be yours; since He always abides with those who, tearing themselves away from all creatures and from themselves, give themselves up entirely, and sacrifice themselves to His Divine Majesty.

Here then, beloved, you see a most powerful way of overcoming all your enemies; because if this offering so unites you to God, that you become wholly His, and He wholly yours, what enemy and what power can ever hurt you? And when you wish to offer to Him any of your works, as fasts, prayers, acts of patience, or any other good deeds, first turn your mind to the offering which Christ made to the Father of His fasts, prayers, and other works; and in trustful dependence on the worth and virtue of these, offer then your own.

When you wish to offer to your Heavenly Father the works of Christ, in satisfaction for your sins, you will do it in this manner. You will make a general, and sometimes a particular, review of your sins, and seeing clearly that it is not possible for you, of yourself, to appease the anger of God, nor to satisfy His Divine Justice, you will have recourse to the Life and Passion of His Son, and meditate upon some one of His actions; as, for example, when He fasted, prayed, suffered, and shed His Blood; here you will see that, in order to propitiate the Father, and to pay the debt of your iniquity, He offered Him these His Works, His Suffering and Blood—as it were saying: "Behold, Eternal Father, what superabundant satisfaction I make to Thy Justice for the sins and trespasses of N. May it please Thy Divine Majesty to forgive them, and to receive that person into the number of Thine elect."

Then make the same offering, and offer these prayers for yourself, to the Father Himself, imploring Him that, by virtue of them, He would forgive you every debt. And this you can do, not only by passing from one Mystery to another, but also from one act to another in the same Mystery;

and this mode of offering may serve not only for yourself, but also for others.

CHAPTER 59

Of Sensible Devotion and of Dryness.

SENSIBLE devotion arises sometimes from nature, sometimes from the devil, and sometimes from grace. You will be able from its fruits to discern its source; since if it does not produce amendment of life, your only doubt will be, whether it proceeds from the devil, or from nature; and especially, if it is accompanied by a greater relish and sweetness, and attachment, and a certain self-esteem.

When, therefore, you shall feel your mind filled with spiritual sweetness, do not stop to dispute about the source from whence it comes; and do not lean upon it, nor suffer yourself to be taken off from the thought of your own nothingness; but with greater diligence and hatred of self, study to keep your heart free from all attachment, even to spiritual things, and seek God alone, and His good pleasure; for in this way the delight—whether it spring from nature or from the devil—will be changed into an effect of grace to you.

Dryness may likewise proceed from these three causes.

From the devil, to make the mind lukewarm, and to cause it to turn from spiritual exertion to the occupations and delights of the world.

From ourselves, through our faults, earthly attachments, and neglects.

From grace, either to give us warning, that we should be more diligent to forsake every attachment and employment which is not of God, and does not terminate in Him; or, to make us learn by experience, that all our good things come from Him; or, that we may for the future more highly esteem His gifts, and be more humble and cautious in preserving them; or, that we may unite ourselves more closely to His Divine Majesty with entire self-renunciation even as to spiritual delights, that our affections may not be so attached to them as to divide the heart which the Lord would have wholly for Himself; or else, because He is pleased to see us put forth all our strength in battle, and use His grace.

If you then should feel dry, enter into yourself, that you may discover from what fault of your own you have been deprived of sensible devotion; and against it make war, not with the motive of recovering a consciousness of grace, but in order that you may remove what is displeasing to God.

And if you cannot find out the fault, let your sensible devotion be true devotion, which is prompt resignation to the Will of God. But on no account leave off any of your devotions, but pursue them with all your might, however fruitless and distasteful they may appear to you; drinking willingly the cup of bitterness, which in this dryness the loving Will of God holds out to you.

And if at times dryness is accompanied with such great and thick darkness of mind, that you neither know which way to turn, nor what step to take, yet be not dismayed, remain alone and firm upon the Cross, far from every earthly delight, even though it should be offered you by the world or by any creature.

Conceal your suffering from every one except your spiritual father, and disclose it to him, not with a view of alleviating pain, but in order to learn how to bear it according to God's pleasure.

Let Communion, prayer, and other exercises be used, not that you may come down from the cross, but to receive the strength to exalt that cross to the greater glory of the Crucified. And when you are unable to meditate, through confusion of mind, and cannot pray as usual, meditate as best you can. And what you cannot accomplish with the understanding, make a violent effort to effect with the will and with words, holding converse with yourself, and with your Lord; for this will have wonderful effects, and thus your heart will gain breath and strength.

You can then in such a case say: "Why art thou cast down, O my soul? and why art thou disquieted within me? hope thou in God: for I shall yet praise Him, Who is the health of my countenance, and my God." "Why stand Thou so far off, O Lord, and hide Thy Face in the needful time of trouble? Forsake me not utterly."

And remembering the sacred teaching which God imparted in time of tribulation to His beloved Sarah, the wife of Tobias, make use of it also, and say aloud: "But whoso serves Thee knows assuredly, that his life, if passed in trial, will be crowned; if in tribulation, will be freed; and if in chastisement, he may fly to Thy Mercy. For Thou delight not in our destruction; for Thou make a calm to succeed a storm, and after tears and weeping, Thou infuse joy. Be Thy Name, O God of Israel, blessed for ever!" *Tob.* iii.

You will remember also your Christ, Who, in the Garden and on the Cross, was, to His great pain, abandoned by His Heavenly Father, as far as the feeling of comfort was concerned; and, bearing the cross with Him, with all your heart say, "Thy Will be done." By doing so, your patience and prayer will raise the flame of your heart's sacrifice into the presence of God, leaving you truly devout; true devotion (as I have said to you) consisting in a lively and firm readiness of will to follow Christ with the cross on your shoulder, by whatever way He invites and calls us to Himself, to desire God for God, and at times to leave God for God.

And if by this, and not by devotional feelings, many persons (and especially women), who aim at a spiritual life, would measure their progress, they would not be deceived by themselves nor by the devil, nor would they uselessly, or rather ungratefully, complain of so much good which the Lord has done them; but they would strive with greater earnestness to serve His Divine Majesty, Who disposes and permits all things for His Glory, and our good.

And here, again, do women deceive themselves, who guard themselves with fear and prudence from every occasion of sin; but when at times they are molested by horrible, filthy, and fearful thoughts, and also sometimes by most loathsome visions, they are confounded, and lose heart, and make themselves believe that they are forsaken by, and wholly banished from God, and cannot persuade themselves that the Holy Spirit can abide in a mind filled with such thoughts.

Thus, continuing much cast down, they are ready to despair, and, having left all their good exercises, to return to Egypt.

They do not well understand what grace the Lord bestows on them; for He suffers such persons to be assailed by these spirits of temptation, to bring them back to the knowledge of themselves, and in order that, by feeling their need of Him, they may draw near to Him.

Therefore they ungratefully complain of that, for which they ought to feel themselves indebted to His infinite Goodness.

What you ought to do in such cases is, to bring yourself low by the consideration of your perverse inclinations, which, God wills for your good that you should know, are prone to every sin, even the most grievous; and that, without His succor, you would rush to utter ruin.

And from this enter into a state of hope and confidence, and gather that He is ready to help you, since He makes you see the danger, and wishes to draw you nearer to Himself by prayer and by recourse to Him; for this, therefore, you ought to render Him most humble thanks. And be assured that such spirits of temptation and filthy thoughts are better banished by a patient endurance of the pain, and by dexterous diversion of the mind, than by a too anxious resistance.

CHAPTER 60

Of the Examination of Conscience.

IN the examination of conscience consider three things:

The falls of that day;

The cause of them; and,

The energy and promptness which you maintain in making war against them, and in acquiring the contrary virtue.

As to the falls, you will do what I advised you in the chapter on "When we are wounded."

The cause of these falls you will be constrained to subdue and bring to the ground.

The will to do this, and to acquire virtues, must be fortified by distrust of self, by trust in God, by prayer, and by a multitude of acts of hatred of the vice, and of desire for the contrary virtue.

You should suspect the victories and good works you have accomplished.

Besides that, I do not advise you to think much about them, because of the risk, almost inevitable, of at least some hidden motive of vainglory and pride.

Then leave all that is behind, whatever it may be, to the mercy of God, and consider how much yet remains for you to do.

Then, in a strain of thankfulness for the gifts and favors which the Lord has bestowed on you during that day, acknowledge Him as the Doer of all good, and return thanks to Him for having rescued you from so many open enemies, and from so many more hidden ones; for having given you good thoughts, and occasions of virtue, and for all other benefits which you may not have known though you received them.

CHAPTER 61

How in this Battle we have need of continuing the Struggle even unto Death.

AMONGST other things which are in request in this combat, one is the perseverance with which we ought to mortify incessantly our passions, which are never dead in this life; but, on the contrary, like evil weeds, spring up hourly.

And this is a battle which only ends when life ends, so that there is no escape for us from it; for he who does not fight in it, is of necessity either taken captive or killed.

Besides, we have to do with enemies who bear us an unceasing hatred, therefore we can never hope for peace from them, nor for a truce, inasmuch as they slay those most cruelly who most seek to make friends of them.

You have no need, on that account, to fear their power and number, since in this battle no one can be a loser except he wills to be. And the whole strength of our enemies is held in the Hand of our Captain, for Whose honor we have to contend.

He not only will not suffer you to be overborne, but He will even take up arms for you, and, being more powerful than all your adversaries, He will give the victory into your hand; if only you will fight manfully together with Him, and not trust in yourself, but in His Power and Goodness.

And if the Lord does not so quickly grant you the victory, do not lose heart, but be the more certain (and this will help you to fight confidently) that every thing which happens to you—even those which seem most unlikely to lead to, nay, which seem opposed to, victory (of whatever kind they may be)—He will overrule to your good and advantage, if you will only conduct yourself as a faithful and generous warrior.

You then, beloved, following your Heavenly Captain, Who for you has overcome the world, and has willed to die Himself, give yourself with a courageous heart to this battle, and to the utter destruction of all your foes; for if you leave but one alive, he will be as a beam in your eye and a thorn in your side, which will retard you in the course of so glorious a victory.

CHAPTER 62

How to prepare ourselves against the Enemies who assault us when we are Dying.

ALTHOUGH our whole life is a continual warfare on earth, yet the chief and most signal struggle is at the last hour of the great passage, since he who falls at that moment does not rise any more.

This is what you have to do now, that you may be found well prepared then; you must in the present time which is given you fight manfully, for he who fights well in life will, by the good habit which he has already formed, easily gain the victory in his last moments.

Besides this, think often on death with careful consideration, so, when it comes upon you, you will fear it less, and your mind will be free and ready for the conflict.

Worldly men fly from this thought, lest it disturb their delight in earthly things, on which they have willed to set their affections, so that the thought of having to quit them gives them pain. Thus the inordinate affection for them does not diminish, but on the contrary takes more and more possession of them, so that the idea of separation from this life, and from things so dear to them, is unspeakably distressing, and often most so to those who have longest made them their delight.

That you may be able to make this important preparation the better, imagine yourself sometimes to be alone, without any help, and in the anguish of death, and gather before your mind the following things which are likely to give you uneasiness at that time; then think over the remedies, which I shall bring you, so that you may be able to use them the better in that last strait; for the blow which can be given but once should be well learnt beforehand, lest an error be committed which cannot be repaired.

CHAPTER 63

Of Four Assaults of our Enemies at the time of Dying; and first of the Assault upon Faith, and of the Manner of defending ourselves.

THERE are four principal and most dangerous assaults, which our enemies are wont to make against us at the time of death.

They are; temptation of faith, despair, vainglory, and various illusions and transformations of devils into angels of light.

As to the first assault; if the enemy begin to tempt you with his false arguments, retire at once from the understanding to the will, saying: "Get thee behind me, Satan, father of lies, for I will not even hear thee; enough for me to believe what the Holy Catholic Church believes."

And do not, as far as possible, give place to questions about the faith, however plausible they may seem, but regard them as prompted by the devil in order to stir up anxiety.

But if, however, you are not in time to turn your thoughts quite away, stand firm and unmoved, so as not to yield to any reason or authority of Scripture, which the adversary may allege; for all will be garbled, or wrongly quoted or misinterpreted, although it may appear to you to be good, clear, and conclusive.

And if the subtle serpent demands of you what the Catholic Church believes, do not answer him, but seeing his device, and that he only wants to catch you in your words, make an inward act of more lively faith; or else, to make him burst with indignation, reply, that the Holy Catholic Church believes the truth; and if the Evil One should ask in return, "What is the truth?" you reply, "Even that which she believes."

Above all, ever keep your heart intent upon the Crucified, saying: "My God, my Creator and Savior, haste Thou to help me, and forsake me not, that I part not with the truth of the Holy Catholic Faith; and may it please Thee, that as in this faith by Thy grace I was born, so in it, to Thy glory, I may end this mortal life."

CHAPTER 64

Of the Assault of Despair, and its Remedy.

THE second assault, whereby the perverse demon strives to accomplish our overthrow, is the terror which he works in us by the remembrance of our sins, in order that we may cast ourselves headlong into the pit of despair.

In this danger, hold fast this certain rule, that the thoughts of your sins are the result of grace, and for your salvation, when they produce in you humility, sorrow for having offended God, and confidence in His

Goodness. But when the thoughts disquiet you, and render you distrustful and faint-hearted, even though the things seem to you true and enough to lead you to persuade yourself that you are condemned, and that the day of salvation for you is past, convince yourself that they are merely the work of the deceiver; humble yourself the more, and trust the more in God, so that in this way you shall overcome the enemy with his own weapons, and bring glory to the Lord.

Mourn, indeed, over your offence against God, every time it comes to your memory, but yet seek pardon, trusting to His Passion.

And, further, I say to you, that if God Himself should seem to say that you are not of His sheep, yet you ought in nowise to let go your confidence in Him, but humbly say: "You have reason indeed, O my Lord, on account of my sins, to cast me away for ever, but I have greater reason on account of Thy mercy to hope for Thy pardon. Therefore, I ask of Thee the salvation of this miserable creature, condemned by its own sinfulness, but redeemed with the price of Thy blood. I wish Thee, my Redeemer, to save me for Thy own glory; and, with confidence in Thy infinite Mercy, I leave myself entirely in Thy Hands. Do with me as Thou please, for Thou art my only Lord; even if Thou slay me, yet my hope will I keep alive in Thee."

CHAPTER 65

Of the Assault of Vainglory.

THE third assault is of vainglory and presumption. In this matter, you must not permit yourself in any imaginable way to be drawn into the very least complacency in yourself, or in your works. Let your delight be in your Lord Alone, in His Mercy, and in the works of His Life and Passion.

Abase yourself ever more and more in your own eyes, even to your last breath; and of every good deed done by you, which may come before you, recognize God Alone for its Author. Have recourse to Him for help, but do not expect it on account of your own merits, however many and great be the battles in which you have been victorious. Ever preserve a spirit of holy fear, acknowledging sincerely that all your precautions would be in vain, if God did not gather you under the shadow of His wings, in Whose protection alone you will confide.

By following this advice, your enemies shall not be able to prevail against you. And thus will you open the road which will lead you joyfully to the Heavenly Jerusalem.

CHAPTER 66

Of the Assault of Illusions and False Appearances at the point of Death.

IF our obstinate enemy, who is never tired of troubling us, assails you by false appearances, by transformations of himself into an angel of light, stand firm and unshaken in the knowledge of your own nothingness, and say to him daringly: "Return, unhappy one, into your darkness, for I am unworthy of visions, nor have I need of anything but the Mercy of my Jesus, and the prayers of the Virgin Mary, of St. Joseph, and of the other Saints."

And if, nevertheless, it appears to you that these things come from Heaven, by many almost convincing signs, yet refuse them, and drive them as far as possible from you. Fear not lest this resistance, founded on your own unworthiness, be displeasing to the Lord; since if the thing be from Him, He knows how to make it clear to you, and you will lose nothing; because He Who gives grace to the humble, does not withdraw it for acts which are done through humility.

These are the weapons which the enemy most commonly employs against us in our last journey.

He tempts each one according to his particular bent—in that to which he knows him to be most inclined. Therefore, before the hour of the great conflict approaches, we ought to arm ourselves well, and fight valiantly against our strongest passions, and against those which have the greatest mastery over us; so that the victory may be easier in that time, which will leave us no other time for action afterwards.

"Fight against them, until they be consumed." 1 *Sam.* xv. 18. 1

THE END